Praise for
When God Writes Your Love Story

"If you're looking for practical ways to build a God-honoring relationship, you can't afford to miss this book."

> —DRS. LES AND LESLIE PARROTT, authors of *Saving Your Marriage Before It Starts*

"Straightforward and unabashed, *When God Writes Your Love Story* delves deep into the Christian single's love life. Take a moment to gain a new perspective on true romance God's way!"

> —BEVERLY LAHAYE, founder and chairwoman of Concerned Women for America

"*Creative, challenging, intuitive,* and *inspirational* are just four of the dozens of exuberant adjectives that fill my heart as I read the you'll-never-be-the-same writings of Eric and Leslie. If you'd like to save the world one more broken heart or fill a heart that is budding with love, secure a copy of *When God Writes Your Love Story* and give one to a special friend."

> —DR. JOE WHITE, president of Kanakuk Kamps

when God writes your love story

EXPANDED EDITION

the ultimate guide to guy/girl relationships

ERIC & LESLIE LUDY

MULTNOMAH
BOOKS

WHEN GOD WRITES YOUR LOVE STORY
PUBLISHED BY MULTNOMAH BOOKS
12265 Oracle Boulevard, Suite 200
Colorado Springs, Colorado 80921

All Scripture quotations, unless otherwise indicated, are taken from the New King James Version®. Copyright © 1982 by Thomas Nelson, Inc. Used by permission. All rights reserved. Scripture quotations marked (NASB) are taken from the New American Standard Bible®. © Copyright The Lockman Foundation 1960, 1962, 1963, 1968, 1971, 1972, 1973, 1975, 1977, 1995. Used by permission. (www.Lockman.org). Scripture quotations marked (ESV) are taken from The Holy Bible, English Standard Version, copyright © 2001 by Crossway Bibles, a division of Good News Publishers. Used by permission. All rights reserved. Scripture quotations marked (NLT) are taken from the Holy Bible, New Living Translation, copyright © 1996. Used by permission of Tyndale House Publishers Inc., Wheaton, Illinois 60189. All rights reserved.

Details in some anecdotes and stories have been changed to protect the identities of the persons involved.

ISBN 978-1-60142-165-4

ISBN 978-1-60142-242-2 (electronic)

Copyright © 1999, 2004, 2009 by Winston and Brooks, Inc.

Published in association with Loyal Arts Literary Agency, LoyalArts.com.

Published in the United States by WaterBrook Multnomah, an imprint of The Crown Publishing Group, a division of Random House Inc., New York.

MULTNOMAH and its mountain colophon are registered trademarks of Random House Inc.

Library of Congress Cataloging-in-Publication Data
Ludy, Eric.
    When God writes your love story : the ultimate approach to guy/girl relationships / Eric & Leslie Ludy. — [Rev. ed.].
        p. cm.
    Includes bibliographical references.
    ISBN: 978-1-60142-165-4 — ISBN 978-1-60142-242-2 (electronic)
  1. Christian youth—Religious life. 2. Courtship—Religious aspects—Christianity. 3. Dating (Social customs)—Religious aspects—Christianity. I. Ludy, Leslie. II. Title.
    BV4531.3.L835 2009
    241'.6765—dc22

                                    2009004352

Printed in the United States of America
2011

10 9 8

Special Sales: Most WaterBrook Multnomah books are available in special quantity discounts when purchased in bulk by corporations, organizations, and special-interest groups. Custom imprinting or excerpting can also be done to fit special needs. For information, please e-mail SpecialMarkets@WaterBrookMultnomah.com or call 1-800-603-7051.

For anyone who has longed to sing the sweeter song.

Contents

Part 3: The Training Ground

Practical Preparation for a God-Written Love Story

Part 4: Happily Ever After
Finding a Real-Life Fairy Tale in the Midst of Modern Reality

Author's Note

⚔ ERIC ⚔

find it kind of strange being an author. It's bewildering that people actually read our books. Don't get me wrong; that *is* why we write them. But it's a strange sensation to realize that somehow the way we personally articulate ideas meshes with the way someone else understands ideas. It's a wonder of wonders that never ceases to amaze us.

This particular book is the one that has surprised me the most because it has received a greater response than all of our other books combined. Ten years ago, *When God Writes Your Love Story* introduced a generation to the extraordinary beauty of a God-scripted romance.

Over the past decade, informal surveys of our readers have shown that an average of five people read each purchased copy of *When God Writes Your Love Story.* It's one of those life-changing books that people like to pass around to their friends. I can't tell you how many faded, battered, torn-up copies of this book I've signed over the years. I love signing the really bedraggled copies, those "I've read it seventeen times" copies.

This book has somehow, through all its quirky stories and romantic nit-witticisms, effectively wormed its way into the hearts of countless readers and is still one of the greatest-selling Christian relationship books of all time. I may not be able to fully comprehend the reasons for that, but something packaged inside this book has deeply moved hundreds of thousands of people to completely alter their approach to building romantic relationships.

And I think that response comes, at least in part, because the message is so simple. Well, it also might have to do with the fact that this book hews tightly to the triumvirate of qualities that characterize every classic Ludy book: it's desperately romantic, awkwardly hilarious, and of course, spiritually heartwarming.

To be quite honest, both Leslie and I felt a longing to completely rewrite this book from scratch. We were convinced we could express the message so much better and more profoundly now that we have ten years of added wisdom under our belts. However, when we presented that idea to a few of the more vocal members of the *When God Writes* fan club, they were all quite disturbed by the concept.

One individual proclaimed, "Don't mess with this book! It's Eric and Leslie captured in a bottle, with all their youthful zeal, naiveté, corniness, and passion fully intact."

While Leslie and I were inclined to make this book sound a bit more grown-up, it would seem that the eccentric youthful nature of this book is part of its magic. It's a hilarious book about some of the most dead-serious issues on planet Earth. And somehow, it works. So instead of changing the whole book, we did as our publisher asked and just "freshened" it up a bit. This revised edition is an update of the classic message that has impacted so many lives.

For those of you familiar with the original version, you will find all sorts of new chunks of gold hidden within; we've added new stories, deeper truths, and a greater wealth of application. And while many of the embarrassingly outmoded phrases and illustrations have been altered to reflect our modern times, we left in a few Eric-isms just so that you can enjoy a good laugh at my expense.

If you are new to this book, welcome. Leslie and I hope and pray that you will find something in this revised edition that connects with your heart just as it has connected with the hundreds of thousands of readers before you.

Ten years may have passed, but the two of us haven't changed a bit when it comes to the message of this book. We are still crazy in love with each other and still ever-smiling proponents of God-built romance. (It's amazing, but this stuff only gets better with time.)

P.S. To take the message of this book even deeper in your life and to find out more about our ministry, Leslie and I invite you to visit our Web site, www.setapartlife.com. Hope to see you there!

The Awakening

✕ LESLIE ✕

'll never forget the night Brandon broke up with me. Though it happened more than sixteen years ago, the intensity of that experience remains seared upon my memory even now. It was my sophomore year in high school. I was happy and thriving—with plenty of friends and a good-looking, popular boyfriend who seemed to worship the ground I walked on. Life was fun and fulfilling. And then, within the space of a five-minute phone conversation, my world came crashing down around me.

"I think we should break up," Brandon told me, with a matter-of-factness that dug into me like a knife.

My trembling fingers tightened around the phone cord, and I choked back the sob that threatened to explode from my tightening lungs. This didn't make sense. Hadn't he said he would always love me? Hadn't he told me, time and time again, that he could never live without me? Didn't he appreciate the fact that I had built my entire world around him for the past eight months? Didn't he remember the countless hours we had spent together, declaring our devotion and love for each other and selecting names for our future children?

The nightmare had come true again. A relationship that had become my entire identity, security, and source of fulfillment was being ruthlessly ripped away, leaving me heartbroken and devastated.

A cutting pain squeezed my heart, so intense I could scarcely breathe. Somehow I managed to end the phone call with at least a small amount of dignity. As I placed the receiver into its cradle, a dark cloud of despair overcame me, mercilessly pouring a torrent of rejection and hopelessness into my reeling mind.

It was over.

Once again, I was in for a sleepless night of agony, hours of weeping until no more tears would come. Once again, I would have to face the aching, desperate loneliness of walking into a crowded room full of strangers—with no hand to hold, no strong arm to gently rest on my back and give me security. Once again, I was alone.

During the past few years, I had made incredible sacrifices in an attempt to somehow cling to every short-lived dating relationship that came my way. I had given pieces of myself away to each guy that came into my life—pieces of my heart, my emotions, and even my body. Yet each time, once he got bored with me, my fragile heart would be carelessly tossed aside. I longed to be loved and cherished. I had dreamed of a perfect love story ever since I was a five-year-old girl watching *Cinderella*. But somewhere in the midst of the endless cycle of one temporary romance after the next, my dreams had shattered right along with the broken and fragmented pieces of my heart. Yes, I was still young. But even so, I'd already begun to give up on the idea of ever finding real love.

Growing up in church, I had listened carefully to the instructions given by my youth group leaders and tried to follow the Christian rules of dating to the letter. But those rules failed to protect me from a broken heart and shattered life. And as I observed my Christian friends, I saw we were all following the same pattern: an endless cycle of shallow and cheap romances that never lasted and left us emotionally bleeding and insecure.

My desperation finally motivated me to start praying. I'd been a Christian from the time I was five, but in the past few years God had taken a backseat in my life. I would have said that He was my highest priority, but in reality, I was far more preoccupied with guys, friends, and my social status. I didn't really see anything wrong with the way I'd chosen to live. My lifestyle was far more moral than that of most of my peers. Even though God wasn't the centerpiece of my daily life, I assumed that I was still on good terms with Him.

But the fact that I kept getting my heart broken again and again finally made me wonder if I was doing something wrong. A few days after the Brandon breakup, still wallowing in depression and confusion, I cried out to God.

"What am I doing wrong?" I asked earnestly. "I've followed the Christian dating rules. I'm not having sex before marriage, and I'm dating Christian guys. Why am I so miserable and insecure? Why does every relationship end this way?"

Then came a soft tugging upon my heart. Suddenly I somehow knew that my life did not need to be this way and that God had something better for me. I felt Him gently whisper these words to my soul: *You continue to get your heart broken because you are holding the pen of your life and trying to write your own story. I am the Author of true love.*

I am the Creator of romance. I know your heart's every desire. I want to script a beautiful tale just for you, but first you must give the pen to Me. You must let Me become the center of your existence. You must let Me have total control of your love life, and every other area of your life as well.

The thought of giving God complete control of my life, especially my love life, was a bit daunting. I didn't really mind obeying certain Christian guidelines for dating, as long as I could still hold the pen and write the story myself. But...letting go of my right to make all my own decisions about relationships? I just wasn't sure I was ready to give God *that* much control. God was asking me to trust Him—fully, completely, and wholeheartedly. He was asking me to allow Him to write my love story. But what if He let me down? Even though my Sunday school upbringing had taught me that God loved me, inwardly I always suspected that maybe He was more interested in making me miserable than in blessing me. What if I gave Him the pen and He completely destroyed this area of my life? What if He never allowed me to find a love story at all? Or what if He directed me to someone I wasn't even attracted to?

I wrestled intensely with the decision. And in spite of all my fears and misgivings about turning the pen of my life over to God, one realization was extremely clear. As long as I continued writing my own story, I knew I would only find more heartache and disappointment. I had made a mess of this area of my life thus far. It was clear I needed some serious help.

So, more out of desperation than confidence, I invited the Creator of the universe to be the center of my love life. Did He disappoint me? Just the opposite. I was soon to discover that the Author of love and romance, who loved me more than I could comprehend, had a plan for my love life that would take my breath away with its beauty.

I don't know if I could ever fully convey the wonder of what it was like to have a God-written love story. During my entire pre-marriage relationship with Eric, I was so aware of the fact that it was *God* who was leading each step, guiding each conversation, painting each sunset, and standing over us with a smile. The cheap, imitation romance I'd known before simply could not be compared to this new kind of love. Daily I was amazed that I had come from a place of heartbreak, confusion, and compromise in relationships to a dream come true. I discovered a kind of divine love that can't even be found in the fairy tales, simply by giving God the pen of my life's story and allowing Him to write each chapter.

In this day and age of do-it-yourself Christianity, many scoff at the idea of God scripting a love story. Countless Christian voices caution that we shouldn't allow our expectations of Him to become too high or we'll only be disappointed.

In fact, it's often deemed more spiritual to take matters into our own hands, make all our own decisions, and then ask God to bless our choices. And that's the

> *As for God, His way is perfect.*
> PSALM 18:30

way most modern Christians have chosen to approach this area of life. Ever since Eric and I began speaking about God-written love stories, we've heard the response, "Well, maybe you two experienced that, but I don't know very many other people who have! I don't think it's something that everyone should expect."

It's true that God-scripted love stories are not common in today's world. But the reason is that so few of us are truly willing to *allow* God to have His way in our lives. As long as *we* are in control, we don't give Him the opportunity to prove just how interested He is in this precious area of our lives. Eric and I strongly believe that if you are brave enough to turn the pen of your life over to the Author of romance, you'll soon discover that God *is* in the business of scripting fairy-tale love stories. (And yes, this is true even if He's called you to a life of singleness, as we'll discuss later on.) God's version of building a relationship is infinitely superior to the pattern this world offers. God doesn't need to imitate the world's method for writing a love story; He has His own version. And once you find yourself in the pages of His captivating script, you'll never want to go back to the mediocre romances of our modern times!

This book contains a message that can forever alter your life. I invite you to join Eric and me as we share with you the incredible process of discovering a God-written love story. No matter what you've been through in relationships, no matter how cynical you might be, this message is for you. God is intensely interested in this area of your life. If you choose to trust Him with absolute abandon, you will discover something beyond all you've ever dreamed of.

This book is not about rules or relationship how-tos. It's not a comprehensive guide to experiencing the singles scene or making yourself more appealing to the opposite sex.

Rather, this book is an invitation. The One who knows you better than you know yourself, and who loves you more than you can comprehend, wants to take you on a journey.

This journey is for anyone who is searching for the beauty of true and lasting love, for romance in its purest form, and who is willing to do whatever it takes to find it. This journey is for anyone who has made mistakes and said, "It's too late for me to discover *that* kind of love." It's a journey for anyone who is tired of the same old scene of physically intense relationships devoid of meaning and purpose.

This journey is for anyone who will dare to dream beyond the cheap and diluted romance our culture offers and hold out for an infinitely better way. This journey is even for the skeptic who doubts that such a way exists.

No matter where you are or where you have been, *this invitation is for you.* The Author of all true love and romance stands before you, asking, *Will you let Me write your love story?*

Part One

The Author
of Romance

Giving God the Pen

One

The Babes and the Big Egos

The day I made my choice

✕ ERIC ✕

All the Kens and Barbies sat around the table.[1] Amid glistening smiles and Coppertone tans, the fragrance of Polo with a hint of Skin So Soft (yes, this was the good old nineties!) wafted through the café booth. I nibbled at my burrito as the conversation around me finally arrived at its ultimate destination.

"So, Kevin," Barbie no. 1 flirted across the table, "tell us who you're seeing now."

Kevin, the son of a state senator, was used to having eyes upon him. Being a Tom Cruise look-alike has a way of boosting the ego. As he crunched a chip between perfect teeth, an "I thought you'd never ask" smirk found its way across his face.

As all of us camp counselors leaned in, eyes bulging with

expectancy, Kevin finally revealed the secret in a low monotone: "Her name is…Sandra!"

This only added to the excitement and wonder, because no one had any idea who Sandra was.

"Is she a babe?" crooned the resident Brad Pitt, alias Mike from Wyoming.

Say no more! Swift as the bionic man, Kevin whipped out his wallet. Moments later we all observed a photograph of the "hottest girl on the planet," as Kevin so proudly referred to her.

"Niiice!" came the rumble of approval from Brad Pitt and Matt Damon (Wayne from Denver).

"*I* think she has a huge nose!" grumbled one of the girls under her breath.

I continued to pick at my burrito.

Barbie no. 2, sitting beside Top Gun, was next in the heartthrob inquisition. She displayed a photo of her boyfriend to cheers of "You go, girl!" from the Barbies and disapproving rumbles about his skinny neck from the Kens, Brads, Matts, and Toms.

After a week of having to exhibit saintlike behavior to all the little campers and being superspiritual while around the camp leaders, it was time to let our hair down—time to let the real passions of life come out. I mean, in your late teens and early twenties, you can sing only so many spiritual camp songs before you need an infusion of good old-fashioned romance.

One year earlier, talks like this had really lit my fire. I used to love to brag about my love life at camp and exaggerate about *my* "sexy new girlfriend" in a way that would make all the guys jealous and all the girls insecure. You could say just about anything and get away with it; no one was going home with you to check out your story.

I used to crave these love life chats, but something about Eric Ludy had changed—something big. Something that made me want to slide under the table when all those inquisitive eyes turned my way.

I'll never forget the moment. There I was, my fork poking at the jalapeño stranded on the corner of my plate and my mind screaming over and over, *Please don't ask me…please don't ask me.*

They asked.

"So, Eric, tell us about your exciting love life!"

All the periwinkle, emerald, and dark brown eyes were twinkling at me with expectation. I gulped.

"Uh," I mumbled. My palms were sweaty. My tongue was dry and thick, like I had a felt eraser in my mouth. Finally, I found my voice. "Uh, I uh, actually, uh, I am waiting on God."

But to be honest, it didn't really come out as clearly as I just wrote it. The last part of my sentence was mumbled under my breath, sounding something like, "Ima waying on Gaw."

I hoped a brief answer would encourage them to move on to Elle Macpherson (a.k.a. Kayla from Utah) seated next to me, poised and ready with a photo of her hunk. The plan backfired. They became even more interested.

"Uh, I think we missed that, Ludy," Tom Cruise sarcastically challenged. "Was that a girl's name or some kind of Chinese food?"

After the laughs subsided, I began again, this time a little more clearly.

"I know this may sound strange, you guys, but I've decided that

I won't give my heart to another girl until God shows me it's my wife."

I have often wished I could have been more eloquent, that I could have made my resolve sound a little more appealing to my audience, now staring at me with mouths ajar. But I guess God wanted me to know that I was following a different path, that I was not to seek the approval of the Kens and Barbies of this world but simply to honor and love Him.

It was a lonely moment. Silence filled our corner of the restaurant, and all eyes focused on the jalapeño I was ruthlessly stabbing to death.

"That's…interesting!" Barbie no. 1 awkwardly noted, her eyes large with disbelief.

Wayne from Denver was not quite as subtle in his disapproval. "Oh, give me a break!" he exploded in disgust. "How in the world do you expect to find someone, Ludy, if you're not out there looking?" His words incited a chorus of *yeahs* and *exactlys* from around the booth.

After a moment of reflective silence, I took a deep breath and stated, "I believe that if God wants me to be married"—another deep breath—"He will pick her out for me."

A dark cloud settled over the entire group and rained down bewilderment in the form of pursed lips and rolled eyes. I glanced up from my tortured jalapeño to discover a long bony index finger pointing at me, about twelve inches from my nose. Kevin used that finger like Clint Eastwood used a gun. He didn't shoot to maim—he shot to kill. His bronzed face had turned red with annoyance, and his lips were quivering with indignation, like a lava pool ready to explode. After three long seconds, he finally erupted.

"I totally disagree with you!" he fumed, his index finger still targeting my right nostril. "God doesn't want us hanging around nagging Him about something like *that!*"

A few "amens" from the crowd textured his passionate sermon. He continued. "I believe God wants *us* to pick," he preached, "and then He blesses *our* choice!" He paused and then came to a climactic finish: "It's sappy Christianity like yours that gives us Christians the image of helpless orphans! It is absolutely *ridiculous* to think that God would care that much about *your* love life!"

The finger held fast for another few long seconds, then slowly dropped as if to say, *You show any sign of life, and I'll shoot again!*

I was the ultimate bummer to their titillating conversation. If ever you want to drain the juice right out of romance, just bring God into the picture. I had committed the unpardonable camp counselor sin, and all the eyes around the table were letting me know it.

Growing up, I had always gotten along with everybody. I knew how to be liked by the crowd and not offend anyone. I was careful to say the right thing in order to avoid disagreements. Eric Ludy had never been known for his backbone...well, except maybe in championing the Denver Broncos. But when it came to things that *really* mattered, I was just plain spineless. This was one of the first times in my life I can remember actually standing up for something I believed in (that wasn't orange and blue).

Ironically, I didn't even know exactly what I was talking about. Just twelve months before, I, too, would have "totally disagreed" with what I had just said. But over the past year, God had been challenging me to apply my Christianity to *every* area of my life. Was it ridiculous to think God would be interested enough in my love life to direct me to the girl He wanted me to spend my life with?

I shifted in my seat, stabbed my jalapeño one last time, and spoke. "All I know," I said, "is that every time I've tried to find someone myself, I realize in the long run that I have horrible taste."

All eyes were wide with amazement as I concluded, "Kevin, if God had ten women line up in front of me and said, 'Eric, you pick,' I would fall flat on my face before Him and say, 'God, You know me better than I know myself... *You pick!*' "

I'll bet no one present other than myself remembers that scene. To them it was probably just the ramblings of a lunatic named Ludy. But for me it was a defining moment. It was almost as if God was saying, "How seriously are you going to trust Me, Eric?"

So there it was, in front of the babes and the big egos, that God challenged me to officially trust Him with the pen of my life. I had held onto that pen for twenty years, and now, over a chicken burrito and a mangled jalapeño, I handed it over to the great Author to allow Him to work His wonders.

I've never regretted it for a moment.

Two

The Sweeter Song

A generation's longing for a better kind of love

⁂ ERIC ⁂

Senior year homecoming was a disaster. Some wacko played upon my gullibility and convinced me that in October, Jesus would return and the end of the world would come.

Why I believed this guy, I'll never know. But for some reason I was convinced that within a very short time, I would be caught up in the clouds for all of eternity. Due to the fact that the world was only weeks away from total devastation, I had to put my priorities right in my life.

The homecoming dance was a month away, and a good majority of the girls were still available. *I'm not even going to be around for that,* I reasoned to myself as the weeks ticked away. The problem was, not only did the weeks pass by without Jesus returning, but all the available dates from my school were snatched up by other guys less concerned about the world's impending destruction.

Well, life would just have to continue. The homecoming dance could go on without old dateless Eric...except for one small problem. Much to my shock, I somehow ended up in the homecoming court. Now I *had* to go. And I had to have a date.

I found a girl in a nearby town who was a friend of a friend. She agreed, rather reluctantly, to be my date for the evening. But she made her feelings clear: "The fact that I'm going with you to this party doesn't mean anything beyond going to this party, I hope you know!"

She was a curly-headed brunette, heavy on perfume and light on charm. Of course, I'm sure that my gross insensitivity to her throughout the evening did not draw out her best side. My first mistake was forgetting her at the dance and losing her for about an hour. The second mistake I made sort of sealed my fate for the evening. It was all very innocent. There I was, fumbling around trying to somehow apologize for my complete lack of sensitivity. I mean, I hadn't just forgotten that she was with me that night; I had totally forgotten that she existed until another girl came up and informed me, "Brandy is furious with you!"

I innocently replied, "Who's Brandy?"

So there I was, brainless as a paperweight and red as a beet, trying to convince my date that she was important to me.

"Brandy," I floundered, "you are great! You are special!"

She looked at me and snorted in disgust. Then came my demise. Over the next few minutes, my buddies crowded around, and the conversation began to brighten. A few jokes were made, and all of us were laughing. Well, all except Brandy. My buddy Darren brought up the subject of names, and we were chuckling about how all of us sort of take on an appearance that fits our names. That was my cue. Brilliant Don Juan that I was, I turned my gaze toward my date and spoke.

"It's kinda hilarious, but did I tell you…I've got an arthritic old cat named Brandy?!"

Her eyes narrowed, and she replied dryly, "Really? Well, I have a pug-nosed dog named Eric!"

That was the last I ever saw of poor Brandy.

The Beautiful Side of Love

Most of us have fallen flat on our faces when it comes to romance. Nearly all of us are familiar with the awful fragrance that accompanies a decomposing relationship.

As Joel, a college friend, said after he had crashed and burned once again on a Saturday night, "Man! I know how to start the relationships; I just don't know how to keep 'em."

That, unfortunately, is not a problem isolated to Joel from the third floor of Baker Hall (who, by the way, is still single as of the last romance update). In our generation it is a problem of epidemic proportions.

Then there is Margo from Minnesota. Margo doesn't feel much sympathy for Joel. As she would say, "I wish I even had the *opportunity* to mess up a relationship with a guy!"

Whether you identify with Joel or with Margo or neither, I guarantee you will identify with the sentiments of Katie, a senior in college who has done a lot of thinking on the subject. "Eric and Leslie, my greatest desire," Katie told us with great passion, "is that my love story would be beautiful."

Katie represents the sentiments of an entire love-hungry genera-tion weaned on condoms and AIDS education. We know the biology, but we do not know "the beautiful side of love."

If we were to be honest, most of us concluded by the age of six-teen that the "beautiful side of love" is something only discovered on an old-fashioned Hollywood movie set by people like Cary Grant and Grace Kelly.

I know the world you live in, because I live in it too. And although I didn't get a doctoral degree in romance, I believe that Leslie and I have a message that can turn your concept of a love life upside down. If you're anything like the rest of this love-hungry generation, you are going to discover a little taste of heaven on earth when you read about the "beautiful side of love" that *really does* exist.

If you knew my love life's history, you might wonder what quali-fies me to share this beautiful side of love with you. I often wonder the very same thing. From the beginning, I was quite inept at this relationship thing. I had my gangly, four-eyed, brace-faced season of struggle, when I was termed by all the well-meaning women in my life as "skinny" and in desperate need of one of their "fattening up" meals.

No one can accuse me of not knowing what it feels like to be ugly. I remember getting a free photo shoot from Olan Mills when I was at the height of my ugly years. I think they paid *me* to take the photo off their hands just so it would not end up in their example album by mistake.

I also know what it is like to be lonely. In fact, long after the awk-ward and ugly years had passed, I experienced the toxic mix of loneliness and sexual longing that creates the sensation of your heart being toasted like a s'more-destined marshmallow over a roaring campfire.

I know what it is like to want someone to hold, someone to gently lean upon me, someone to care about me more than anyone else on earth. I know what it is like to desire someone with whom I can share my passionate love, my sappy love songs, and my intimate embrace. I know what it is like to long for "the beautiful side of love."

As I said, homecoming 1988 was a disaster. There was nothing beautiful about it. (I'm still a little insecure when people talk about pug-nosed dogs around me.) But wedding date 1994 was off-the-charts incredible! Somewhere between homecoming and honeymoon, my entire understanding of love changed. And in the process, I discovered what is missing in our modern concept of love and romance. I discovered the beautiful side of love. And I found it in a very unexpected place.

Passion and the Pew

Growing up in the church, I came to believe that everything I longed for was somehow bad for my proper spiritual development. "THOU SHALT NOT!" the pastor would boom from the pulpit as I sat in the rear-numbing pew, daydreaming about sexy Suzie McFrougal from Hank's Burger Barn. For most of my life, I thought it was *God* who posed the greatest hurdle to experiencing all the thrills of love and romance. And I would have taken great offense if someone tried to convince me that God should have an even bigger role in my love story. All the stern "thou shalt nots" He had so thoughtfully bestowed on me were quite enough, thank you.

For many years I struggled to find the right words to capture my agonizing frustrations. I was a young man fighting a constant inward battle between needing to obey God's "thou shalt nots" and longing to fulfill my passionate sensual desires.

It wasn't until I stumbled upon the following story from Greek legend that I found the perfect picture to describe my years of torment. If you have unsuccessfully tried to mix "the passion" with "the pew," there's a good chance that you will be able to relate to the hidden message in this classic Greek tale (with a Ludy twist).

A Sweet Song Beckons
(Based on Homer's *Odyssey*)

Captain Ulysses cut a powerful figure as he stood on the deck of his great ship. The afternoon sun shimmered off the water as he strode about the vessel with grace and dignity.

"Steady as she goes!" Ulysses boomed, his voice filling the salty air.

After giving the command, the captain turned his gaze to the starboard side where land was just now coming into view. Neither the screeching gulls overhead nor the rhythmic splash of water against the ship's side diverted Ulysses' attention from what lay just ahead. The smell of adventure was in the air; everything was just as Ulysses liked it. Amidst his reverie a voice arrested his attention.

"Captain!"

The noble leader quickly turned to find a worried seaman, eyes filled with trepidation.

"Captain!" he shouted again, his whole face ablaze with horror.

"Calm down!" Ulysses commanded. "Take a deep breath and tell me what's the matter."

The entire crew within earshot had stopped and gathered 'round to hear the outcome of this all-important conversation.

"Uh…we…uh…," he stuttered.

Ulysses grabbed him by the collar, yanked him within inches of his furrowed brow and demanded, "Come on, lad. If you value your life, speak!"

The drama built as the petrified first mate raised a quivering finger due north and blurted out, "The Sirens, sir!"

Ulysses' face drew tight, and a woeful sigh wafted throughout the ship. The Siren mermaids were just ahead, ready to sing their irresistibly enchanting song and cause the bewitched sailors to steer their vessel onto the rocks. The song of the Sirens was so sweet, so alluring, no red-blooded man could resist it. Ulysses had to act quickly—while wisdom still remained.

"Those devils won't get us!" he announced to his fearful crew. "That's right! That intoxicating music won't have its way with us. No shipwreck for us today, lads!"

But even as Ulysses pondered the mesmerizing music, he felt his wisdom slipping. He was gripped by a magnetic urge to hear just a short strain of the Sirens' legendary song.

Maybe we could just steer away from the rocks, he reasoned. Then he chided himself. *NO! The Sirens' music does this to all captains who pass by. They all think they can resist, but then lose their senses and follow the sweet music to their deaths upon the jagged rocks, while the monsters scoff from above. NO!*

Ulysses ran to the bow of the ship, then turned and bellowed for all the crewmen to hear.

"We are mere men, unable to resist the promise of sweet love in the Sirens' song. They have baited every ship before us with their songs, and every time the ships have crashed against the rocks upon which the Sirens sit. But not this time, my friends. *We* will not fall to their temptation; indeed, we will not even allow ourselves to be tempted!

"I want every sailor to take some of this beeswax and put it in your ears so you can hear nothing. And tie *me* to the mast!"

His crew looked at each other in bewilderment.

"You heard me!" he shouted again. "Tie me to the mast! And tie me tight and fast!"

The sun angrily beat down as the disciplined crew rushed about the ship responding to Ulysses' orders. And none too soon, for almost the moment they had crammed the wax into their ears and finished tying their captain to the mast, the beautiful and enthralling love song of the Siren began to softly fill the air. The Sirens' song, in all its passion and wonder, greeted the ship across the water as a warm fire greets cold hands on a winter's day.

The crew was oblivious—all except Ulysses who, while tied to the mast, had no wax to stop the music. Ulysses' blood ran hot with passion. "Untie me!" he screamed in anguish. "Please untie me! I command you to untie me…please, I beg you."

But the crewmen could not hear and had been commanded not to read his lips. The song grew louder and lovelier, and Ulysses began to scream like a madman for someone to heed his orders and turn the ship toward the source of that sweet, lustful music. Ulysses threatened the plank, Cyclops feedings, and various other forms of torture as the ship passed the Sirens' rocky coastline, and then finally beyond the reach of their song.

An exhausted Ulysses, his face a deep scarlet from the struggle, finally was untied and fell exhausted upon the ship's deck.

"Why?" he moaned with his remaining strength. "Why does it seem that the things I desire most in this life lead to my destruction? Why must I be restrained from something so beautiful? The mast is my savior this day from my headlong craving for that sweet but deadly song of the Siren!"[1]

Rope Burned?

I feel Ulysses' pain! I grew up being taught how to "tie myself to the mast" while listening to the song of temptation at full volume. I heard all the fire and brimstone sermons on "the rocks of death." I had all the manuals on enduring rope burn, and I even read one called *How to Chart Your Course So You Never Hear or See a Siren*.

I also lost my senses a few times during my horribly extended pubescent years. I was sort of a Houdini, the way I could slip out of the rope and escape from that mast without any of the Coast Guard finding out. I was a magician when it came to discovering loopholes in the ropes, and I became a seasoned professional at the fine art of incurring serious boat damage.

Like most guys, I grew up in the boys' locker room. The singular topic of conversation that cluttered the airwaves made it a very educational place. I learned far more about my sexuality in two minutes standing next to Donny Lucero's locker than I did in two hours of scientific lecturing from my dad the night he took me for a drive in our banana-yellow VW Bus and gave me "the Talk."

Desire raged within me to have a female companion, someone I could love and be loved by, someone I could be intimate with. The difference between Donny Lucero's advice and the advice I received from my church on the subject was shocking. Ten bucks says you could guess whose advice I preferred.

I wanted to experience all that Donny described. I wanted to understand it, and not just in theory. The problem was, when I came into church and sat down in the pew, I always heard the same thing: *thou shalt not!* And "thou shalt nots" only go so far with a hormone-infested young man who's looking for loopholes in the rope so he can escape and accidentally-on-purpose steer his love boat as close to the rocks as he can possibly get.

The only reason I maintained a semblance of Christian morality when it came to my sex life was because I thought that God would be furious with me if I did not. As much as I wanted to taste all the pleasures of the world, I didn't relish the idea of going to hell. I obeyed the Christian rules because I had to, not because I wanted to. Meanwhile, I felt utterly deprived, dissatisfied, and miserable. Just like Ulysses, I was tied to the mast, listening to the alluring song of the culture and resenting every inch of the ridiculous rope of morality that held me back from following in Donny's footsteps.

My experience echoes the sentiments of an entire generation of young Christians. Church has taught us well. We know we aren't supposed to have sex with whoever we want, whenever we want. We know that God disapproves of the Sirens' song. So we seem to be left with only two choices: Either we grudgingly obey the Christian rules and remain tied to the mast—and nearly go crazy wishing we could experience sex the way everyone else does. Or we give up altogether and crash against the rocks of sexual compromise—and end up feeling guilty and distant from God.

Well, I'm happy to let you know that there *is* a third alternative. You don't have to stay tied to the mast, and you don't have to crash your ship on the rocks. Let me tell you another Greek story—this one a bit more inspiring.

The Sweeter Song

Not far behind Ulysses and his men came another great ship. These sailors also realized the dangers of the Sirens and the rocks upon which they sat.

"Captain Orpheus," the first mate declared, "the sweet song of the Sirens lies just ahead!"

With that announcement, the crew cheered and the great Orpheus smiled. All around the ship, crewmen's voices rang with excitement. The part of the voyage that they longed for was close at hand. In fact, some on the ship had come along *just* to hear the music.

With a knowing smile, the dauntless captain received a beautifully adorned case from his cabin boy. The acclaimed Orpheus carefully removed the priceless instrument as the crewmen stood nearby with bated breath. Then, with princely grace, he lifted the instrument above his head in a gesture of victory, while the crew around him whistled with enthusiasm.

"Play it, Captain!" cheered the helmsman.

All eyes were riveted to their hero. Captain Orpheus took his stance and began to masterfully play the most perfect music men's ears had ever heard. Each crewman became lost in the reverie of the song.

All too soon the Siren coastline was out of sight and the master musician concluded the song that he himself had composed. Not a single man aboard ship was tempted by the Sirens' melody. In fact, no one even noticed it. Though the Sirens' music was alluring and sweet, the superb Orpheus played for his crew…*a sweeter song.*[2]

A Different Tune

For those of us who have spent years tied to the mast, and for those of us who couldn't bear the allurement and crashed against the rocks, it's time to set sail to a different tune.

In our love-hungry generation we struggle to believe that the "beautiful side of love" really exists. But the truth is, Hollywood can't even touch the version of love that is alive and real in the heart and mind of God. It is the "sweeter song." And when you hear this sweeter song, you, too, will realize that it is ten thousand times more magnificent than your grandest imaginings.

God created us with a desire for companionship. He designed us to intensely long for intimacy—spiritual, emotional, and yes, even physical. He did not make us this way and provide us with these longings as a form of cruel torture, but as the most perfect gift He could possibly give us. Just as a lover desires to show his adoration by tenderly presenting his bride with a delicate and fragrant rose, so has our Great Lover gifted us with this delicate and wondrous capacity to give and receive love and passion. And once we awaken to this truth, then we will discover that, as the Inventor of romance, He also wants to teach us how to experience it in all its fullness.

If you dream of something eternally sweet and are tired of rope burn, God is eagerly waiting for you to jump aboard His ship so He can play the sweeter song just for you.

> As for God, His way is perfect; the word of the LORD is
> proven; He is a shield to all who trust in Him.
>
> PSALM 18:30

> Eye has not seen, nor ear heard, nor have entered into the
> heart of man the things which God has prepared for those
> who love Him.
>
> 1 CORINTHIANS 2:9

> Bless the LORD, O my soul, and forget not all His bene-
> fits:…Who crowns you with lovingkindness and tender mer-
> cies, Who satisfies your mouth with good things.
>
> PSALM 103:2, 4–5

A Look Inside Your Heart

1. How would you describe "the beautiful side of love"? Where, if anywhere, have you seen a glimpse of this kind of love?

2. When it comes to your love life, do you think God is more interested in "thou shalt nots" or in helping you hear the "sweeter song"?

3. In what ways do you think God's love song differs from the world's? Which version is more appealing to you, and why?

4. Are you willing to allow God's Spirit to reshape your attitude toward love and romance? In what ways, specifically, does your perspective need to change?

A Step Further

Take some time to meditate upon some of the glorious promises of God found in Psalm 34, Psalm 37, Psalm 84, and Psalm 103. As you do, keep in mind that these promises aren't merely poetic-sounding words, but they actually capture God's very heart toward you. We serve a God who genuinely *delights* in giving good and perfect gifts to His children. He is a rewarder of those who diligently seek Him (Hebrews 11:16). Do you really believe and expect that in your own life? If you struggle with doubt, ask His Spirit to equip you with real faith to believe that God is exactly who He says He is and cares about you as much as He says He does. Write down anything you feel He is speaking to your heart. ✕

Three

Who's Captain of Your Love Boat?

Laying the foundation for a God-written love story

✕ ERIC ✕

A great story in Christian history is about the apostle Andrew, one of Jesus's twelve disciples. Andrew was brought in before the Roman governor Aegeas to be reproved for constantly preaching the controversial message of Jesus. The governor threatened, "If you don't stop preaching this message of Jesus and this cross, I'm going to crucify you on one, too!"[1] I don't know about you, but at such a point I would be very tempted to blurt out, "No problem! You want me to shut up? Sure! My lips are closed! Now, why don't we just forget about this whole crucifixion idea?"

Andrew, though, was undaunted. He simply replied, "Sir, I would not have preached about the glory of the cross of Jesus if I was not also willing to die upon it!"

Andrew was immediately taken out and ruthlessly tied to two beams of splintery wood, then set upright to die a slow and painful death. He hung there, in what must have been excruciating pain, for three days, preaching the triumphant message of Jesus and *His* cross the whole while, until he was finally taken home to be with the One he loved more than his very life.

I don't know about you, but growing up I never saw that type of love for Christ, that type of passion for following Him, that type of abandonment of life. As I headed into adulthood, some serious doubts had begun to creep into my mind regarding the accuracy of some of these legendary stories of the faith. *If following Christ is really like that, then how come I never see anyone live like that today?* I wondered.

I used to just accept what I heard in Sunday school. After all, Mrs. Bloomington, my esteemed Sunday school teacher, had said it. How could *she* be wrong? But something caused me to stop accepting. Maybe it was the fact that I was constantly told by my schoolteachers that God wasn't there. Maybe it had something to do with the flimsy moral backbones of so many people who referred to themselves as Christians. Or maybe it was simply that I came to the point in my life where I wanted to go beyond merely accepting and truly *know* for myself, experientially, what I believed in.

Whatever it was, it invited a little mouse of cynicism into my head. And this pesky little rodent scurried around and nibbled away at my innocence and childlike faith. Though my parents and Mrs. Bloomington had taught me well, I became a doubter that such extravagant love for Jesus could be real, a doubter that Jesus was really Someone people would willingly die for.

That little mouse of cynicism is fairly common in our modern Christian world. It has nibbled away at our very concept of who God is and who He wants to be in our lives. What I finally realized is that God is real, whether I believe He is or not. And the day I recognized that, my nettlesome little mouse was caught in an industrial-size rattrap.

Wimpy Christianity Exposed

When I was nineteen and a freshman in college, my ship had a head-on collision with God's ship. And in case you don't already know, let me tell you: when you crash into the living God, the encounter is certain to renovate every square inch of your life's boat.

Growing up, I guess you could say I had a bit of an attitude problem. When I was fifteen I had been taught by my best friend, Blake, how to strut.

"No! No!" Blake had told me. "Do the chin bob, the eye squint, and the swagger all at the same time—not one after the other."

I didn't learn it overnight, but by the age of nineteen, I had it down to a science—how to saunter into a room with cool indifference, how to toy with girls' hearts, and how to make sure that all eyes always turned approvingly toward me. I'd mastered the art of being a Christian without having to really look like one.

I thought I was doing pretty well at this whole Christian thing. I didn't drink (I'd had only a couple swigs), I didn't smoke, I didn't cuss, and I was still (ahem) a virgin. Now there wasn't a soul alive whom I would have told that virgin thing to when I was nineteen, so count yourself privileged. Let's be honest here. Being a male capable of grunt-ing, sweating, and refusing to ask for directions, but not yet having conquered a woman…in our culture, that isn't real manhood at all.

Jesus Christ to me was nothing more than fire insurance. I had long ago found out what I needed to do to make sure I didn't end up in hell.

"You need to *believe,* Eric!" every Christian in my life had told me from the time I was five. "*Believe* that Christ paid the price for your sins upon the cross. Eric, He suffered and died in your place."

So little Eric, at age six, dressed in his favorite marmalade-orange Winnie the Pooh jammies with red Popsicle stain all around his tiny mouth, pronounced that he *beweeved.*

I *believed.* I *believed* that two thousand years ago this guy named Jesus was nailed to a tree. And that He took all my sins upon Himself, and that I could know for certain I wouldn't end up in hell. But if Christianity was so important and I had all the crucial parts covered, why was my life really no different from anyone else who had good morals, grades, manners, and hygiene?

Well, colliding with God unmistakably opened my eyes to the fact that there was more to Christianity than just believing. There was something electrifyingly beautiful that I had never known. I was on the brink of discovering the "sweeter song."

Krissy and the Book

I was reading a book when God's ship crashed into mine. It was a book my sister, Krissy, had given me for Christmas my freshman year in college.

My sister was famous for giving me great Christmas gifts. A Nerf ball when I was eleven, a muscle shirt and some weight-gain powder when I was sixteen. Some of my favorite gifts have come from my sister. But that particular Christmas she seemed to have lost her touch. I tore open the bright red wrapping paper and furrowed my brow in confusion. *Why would my sister give me such an odd gift?* I wondered with irritation. She knew I never read anything other than sports magazines. And besides, this book, in my opinion, had a horrible cover. No way was I ever going to read it.

"I think you'll like it," was all she told me.

That book sat on my shelf, haunting me, for over a month. Krissy seemed to think there was something in that book that I needed. Soon my curiosity got the better of me, and with much reluctance, I picked it up off my bookshelf.

I'll never regret the moment I finally opened *No Compromise: The Life Story of Keith Green* and started reading. My life has never since been the same. The book was about a man in search of Truth. He looked everywhere for it—Eastern religions, various cults, and eventually biblical Christianity. Finally, he found what he was looking for in Jesus Christ.

I remember thinking, "Well, *I* know Jesus Christ too. What's the big deal?"

But soon I had to face the fact that I didn't know Christ the way Keith Green did. He recognized that Jesus had given *everything* for him, and the least he could do in return was give *everything* back to Jesus.

I had never in my life given anything to Jesus. The God of the universe poured out His life for me, and I had never once even considered what my response should be in the face of the most awesome sacrifice in the history of the world.

Deep conviction penetrated my heart. That night, I fell to my knees and cried. I told the Creator of my life, the Lover of my soul, that He had unlimited access to the life of Eric Winston Ludy.

The holy, all-loving, all-powerful, all-mighty, perfectly peaceful and joyful Life of God is waiting to be ours. It is a priceless gift that comes with only one condition: His Life can only be had in exchange for our own. [2]

ERIC LUDY, *GOD'S GIFT TO WOMEN*

In a sense, God boarded my ship that night. It was the ship that *I* had always captained, and now there was a little "who's steering this thing?" dilemma. *I* had always called the shots, charted the course, chosen when to scrub the deck and what detergent to use. I mean, the ship had *my* name on the front. This had always been *my* ship—and now He wanted to assume command.

In His ever-gentle way, He moved into the captain's quarters.

I was okay with Him taking over part of the ship, as long as some rooms on the lower deck remained under *my* jurisdiction. Even after I turned my life over to the rulership of Christ, there were certain areas I clung to and protected, trying with all the strength I had to somehow maintain control over them.

Christianity, defined in very simplistic terms, can be summarized as "me moving *out*, God moving *in*." Which means God had to move into *every* corner of my existence, even the areas I didn't want to let go of.

Eric, He asked me, *are you ready to trust Me at the helm now? If I am Captain, we are going to have to make some changes. And, Eric, these changes need to be made in more than just the captain's quarters.*

Protecting My Ludy Pride

Clank, clank! He was knocking. I had rushed down into my rooms on the lower deck and locked the doors. I didn't know quite what He meant by "more than just the captain's quarters."

What I had to realize is that when Jesus Christ takes over a life, He doesn't just want the helm and the hallways. He wants the entire ship!

Clank, clank! He kept knocking. The first room He was after was a room I felt He had no business tinkering with. *Clank, clank!* As He continued to knock, I asked myself why God would even be interested in such a messy and smelly room. On the outside of the door I'd hung a sign that read Ludy Pride. Inside this room I kept the strut that Blake had taught me, my deep bassy voice, my arrogant attitude, even my hip hairdo.

If God got ahold of this room, I knew the ramifications on my reputation would be disastrous. If He stripped me of all these ingredients to "coolness," all that would be left would be...who I really was. And that was a scary thought.

"God!" I remember arguing, "If You come into this room, I'm going to end up looking like an idiot!"

Then I had a stroke of genius.

"God! Someone may see me looking like an idiot, someone who knows I'm a Christian. You wouldn't want that to happen! That might give You a bad name!"

Have you ever noticed that God never loses a debate?

God made it clear to me that if He were concerned about His reputation, He would not have chosen someone like me to represent Him in the first place. And if He were pursuing popularity, He would not have allowed Himself to be hung naked between two thieves on a cross.

Eric! He was saying, *My strength is made perfect through your weakness* (2 Corinthians 12:9).

That day, I laid down my pride, my reputation, and all the things that I leaned on to make me appealing to the world. I allowed God to have His way—to strip me of all pretense and self-glorifying behavior. Yes, I lost my carefully crafted pop-culture charm. And yes, I did lose some attention and popularity. But I gained something far better: the likeness of Jesus Christ could now be showcased in and through my life. Instead of drawing all eyes to Eric Ludy, it was now my goal to draw all eyes to Jesus Christ. And amazingly, I found that turning attention away from myself and toward Him was an infinitely more fulfilling way to live.

The *Clank, Clanks* Continue

Clank, clank! It seemed as soon as I opened one door, He would begin knocking on another. *Clank, clank!*

"God! I know You're out there," I said from behind deadbolted door number two, "but I just gave You my precious Ludy pride. Can't You go knock on someone else's door for a change?"

Clank, clank!

Room number two was painted orange and blue (Bronco colors), and a life-size poster of John Elway was plastered on the wall. I would come to this room to eat potato chips and scream. On the door hung a sign that read Beware: Rabid Bronco Maniac Inside! For some reason God wanted into this seemingly innocent room.

Clank, clank!

I used to dream in orange and blue. The Denver Broncos were what I lived for. And more than a few times in the past twenty years, I had died for them too. (Just check your handy sports almanac for details.)

When I was growing up, my mom used to tell me, "Eric, if you cheer so loudly for the Denver Broncos, don't you think you should be cheering even louder for Jesus?" That statement didn't go over particularly well when I was sixteen and obnoxiously chanting, "El-Way! El-Way!" But now something inside me was changing. For the first time I recognized that Jesus *was* more worthy of my cheers than John, and *He* deserved first place in my heart.

That day, I gave up my obsession with the Denver Broncos. Rather than giving idol-worship to this team, I began pouring my admiration and devotion into the King of all kings. Once again, I found that as my heart and mind became centered upon Christ instead of the Denver Broncos, my life was incredibly more satisfying. (Not to mention more emotionally stable, now that I didn't live or die based on the outcome of every game.)

One More Room

Clank, clank!

"No way!" I protested from behind door number three while installing an extra deadbolt. "God, I have just given You my reputation and my Broncos; You have no business knocking on *this* door!"

Clank, clank!

"God! You can have anything else; just please leave this room for me!" I pleaded.

Clank, clank!

On the door to this room hung a sign that read Relationships with the Opposite Sex.

If there is one thing in all of life that we feel sure God has no clue about, it's romance. No way was I going to be the fool who trusted God with my love life and ended up a Robinson Crusoe type of guy with a long white beard, shipwrecked on the desert island of singleness. I was convinced that God was very interested in keeping me single, even though He knew I wanted to be married. And I also was convinced that if God did not subject me to singleness, He would do something even worse.

He would place forever at my side…THE BEAST.

I'd been to church! Some funny-looking people sit in those pews. And if God loved *them,* then maybe He was going to call me to love one of them *too!* I could just picture God forcing me to marry someone I wasn't remotely attracted to. I mean, God couldn't possibly know what I really desired in a girl, could He?

Clank, clank!

I know what you're thinking: *Eric, don't let Him in!*

Because you know that if *I* let Him in, you might feel convicted to consider letting Him into this room in *your* life too. To be honest, I really struggled with this one. Not that I didn't struggle with my room of Ludy Pride and my prized Bronco Maniac pad, but this was different. This room was not just a piece of my life; this room *was* my life. I mean, there was not much left to Eric Ludy if you took away what was in this room.

Weeks passed with a *clank, clank!* at the door, night and day. I remember asking myself, *Why, Eric, can't you trust Him?* I finally realized that my lack of trust came directly back to the fact that I didn't truly *know* Him.

If I could have taken just a little peek into God's father-heart—I mean just a *little* peek—I would have seen how much He delights over me, how much He cherishes and adores me. If I could have realized how interested He is in my highest good, I would have flung the door wide open.

I struggled with trusting God because I didn't truly know His nature and character. He created me; He knows me even better than I know myself. Why wouldn't I say to Him, "Not just *this* room, but Lord, I also want You to come into my other ten rooms down the hall!"

If you long for something more than the hit-and-run relationship cycle, something beautiful and meaningful in your life, then I'm going to lay it on the line. You must let go of the captain's position in your life and trust Him. You must give up the little you're hanging onto now to gain something infinitely greater. You must let go of the helm and allow *Him* to lead.

After many weeks, I unlocked the door. It was the single riskiest thing I had ever done in my life. I remember telling God, on my knees with tears brimming in my eyes, "I'm going to trust that You know what You are doing!"

Then, with a trembling heart, I made a commitment to my Captain.

"I'm willing for You to do whatever You want in this area of my life." I swallowed hard, then continued. "I am willing, almighty God, to be single if that's what You desire for me. And, Lord, if you desire me to someday get married, then the next girl I date and give my heart to will be the one You show me is to be my wife!"

Wounded for Heaven's Sake

In my early twenties I saw a video that forever changed me. It wasn't a movie or documentary. It was just a cheap video recording of an elderly, crippled pastor giving a sermon. Onto the fuzzy screen came a weary old man with a face full of wrinkles. I'll never forget hearing his elderly voice shake as he started off his short little talk. His body looked tired and decrepit, yet his eyes radiated a fire and gentleness I had never in my life seen.

I couldn't help but be drawn in. I waited upon every word this wrinkled man spoke as if he were giving me the secret code to unlocking the mysteries of the universe. And in a way…he was.

In all my growing-up years of being a Christian, my eyes had never seen someone so worthy of my respect, my ears had never heard anything so sweet and tender, and my heart had never burned so desperately to know Jesus better.

This old man was different from the preachers I had heard from the pulpit and the dynamic speakers I had heard on the radio. His words penetrated my heart. He said things I had heard before, but it was the sincerity, the gentleness with which he uttered them that touched my soul. He spoke of his life in Romania under Communist dictatorship, his absolute surrender to Jesus, his unwillingness to deny his faith, his fourteen years of imprisonment, and the horrific tortures that he faced as a result.

I longed to have what he had. I knew I did not want the imprisonment and tortures he had faced, but I wanted the sparkling treasure that emanated from *inside* the man. He had something that, to be honest, I hadn't even known existed. He had the ability to view what I would have termed a living hell as the sweetest of blessings. He even referred to those who tortured him as "ones that he learned to love." I could not doubt the fact that what radiated out of him was a treasure gained through tremendous suffering.

Afterward, I could not get this precious man out of my mind. I longed for what he had more than I had ever wanted anything else in my life. This man understood the God of the universe in the same way the apostle Andrew had when he so willingly died for Him. It was real, it was tangible, it was alive today and not just buried in a history book. What I witnessed was indomitable joy, unquenchable love, and mind-boggling peace. But I realized that it came with a price.

Jesus once said this to those closest to Him:

Blessed are the poor in spirit, for theirs is the kingdom of heaven. Blessed are those who mourn, for they shall be comforted. Blessed are the meek, for they shall inherit the earth. (Matthew 5:3–5)

In other words, you're blessed when you are out of options and all you can do is lean on God. Because when you realize your need for God, it is only then that you tap into His immeasurable greatness and goodness. You're blessed when you've been stripped of that which is most precious to you. Only then can you be tenderly embraced by the One most precious to you.

Jesus originally spoke those words in Greek. And the Greek meaning of the word *blessed* is "supremely happy."

Jesus Himself gave us the key to unlocking the treasure chest where the sheet music to the "sweeter song" is held. Remember how I said earlier that something better is out there when it comes to love, but we'll find it in a very unexpected place? Well, the unexpected place is *God Himself.* And to find the "something better," we have to lean on God and be stripped of that which is most precious to us. In a sense, we have to be willing to become vulnerable to *trust* Him if we wish to find security and satisfaction *in* Him. We have to be willing to let go of what little we have to gain the great riches and supreme happiness He offers. And we have to let Him have the helm if we wish to hear the sweeter song.

The "something better" is found in emptying yourself, surrendering to His lead, letting go of your life and all you hold dear, and entrusting *everything* to Him. Because in doing that, you will be tenderly embraced by the sweetest Musician in all the universe and receive your own personal concert.

> *The floods washed away home and mill, all the poor man had in the world. But as he stood on the scene of his loss, after the water had subsided, brokenhearted and discouraged, he saw something shining in the bank which the waters had washed bare. "It looks like gold," he said. It was gold. The flood which had beggared him made him rich.*[3]
>
> HENRY CLAY TRUMBULL

Letting go is not easy for any of us. But Jesus makes it very clear that to go where He is going and to be a part of His wondrous plan we must deny ourselves, pick up our crosses daily, and follow Him (Luke 9:23).

A rough translation of His words might be, "If you are truly serious about being a follower of Me, then each and every day you are going to need to die to *your* way of doing things, trust Me at the helm, and allow Me to captain your ship! That means I can take your ship wherever I see fit. Trust Me, I love you more than you could ever comprehend, and I have your very best in mind."

One of my heroes is a man named Jim Elliot. He not only inspired me in my love story with Leslie, but he inspired me with his abandonment to his Captain, Jesus Christ. I read his words years after his sacrificial death at the hands of the Auca Indians whom he was attempting to reach with the gospel. He simply said this:

He is no fool who gives what he cannot keep to gain what he cannot lose.[4]

To discover life, Jesus says you first have to give it up (see Luke 9:24; John 12:25). Your love life is no different. If you really desire to one day discover the "beautiful side of love," you have to first walk through the "painful side." Just as pouring concrete is not one of the exciting parts of building a house but an essential part, the same is true of building a magnificent romance. Laying your life down is not the fun and enjoyable part; it's the foundation!

If God is going to write your love story, He first needs you to hand over the pen. If God is going to lead your ship to a harbor of romance beyond the dangerous lure of the Sirens, He needs the helm. As Jesus once said to His followers, "Daily you must trust Me; surrendering everything, including the blood in your veins and the breath in your lungs, for Me to do with as I see fit. If you want to join up with Me, you must let Me lead" (Luke 9:23, paraphrase).

If ever you are going to hear the "sweeter song" that God created you to hear, then you're going to have to first open the door to Jesus and let Him have *His* way. And you are going to have to trust that He, as the inventor of romance, knows how to write a beautiful tale!

> Then Jesus said to His disciples, "If anyone desires to come after Me, let him deny himself, and take up his cross, and follow Me."
>
> MATTHEW 16:24

> I die daily.
>
> 1 CORINTHIANS 15:31

> He who abides in Me, and I in him, bears much fruit; for without Me you can do nothing.
>
> JOHN 15:5

> I have been crucified with Christ; it is no longer I who live, but Christ lives in me.
>
> GALATIANS 2:20

A Look Inside Your Heart

1. Who is in control of your life—you or God? Do you tend to make decisions, then ask God to bless them? Or are you truly surrendered to Him and allowing Him to lead? What evidence in your life supports your answer?

2. Which "rooms" in your life, if any, have you been hesitant to give God access to? What's been holding you back?

3. As you think about giving God the pen of your life and letting Him script your love story as He sees fit, what fears and struggles come to mind?

4. Do you truly believe that God is interested in your highest good? What measurable difference would acting on that belief make in your life?

A Step Further

Many people make a "mental" commitment to acknowledge Christ as their Savior. But to truly be a Christian means something far more than that. It's completely letting go of all our selfish agendas, laying down everything we are at the feet of the Lord who died to save us, and giving Him access to every part of our being. As Leonard Ravenhill put it, "What does it mean to be a Christian? Your life is hid with God in Christ. You are bought with a price; you are no longer your own. You have no time of your own, no money of your own. ...Christ must become your complete Master."[5] Prayerfully consider whether that is the reality of your life.

Are you living for your own selfish pursuits, or for God alone? Are you allowing Him access to every corner of your existence, or do you keep some areas "off limits" to Him? These are not questions to answer lightly. Why not take some time now to allow the Spirit of God to penetrate your heart, shine His searchlight upon every nook and cranny of your inner life, and reveal to you all that stands in the way of His amazing plans and purposes for you? And then, let Him give you the strength to surrender to His ruling control every area of your life. It may be the hardest decision of your life, but it's by far the best one you could ever make! ✕

Four

Rules versus Relationship

Discovering the beauty of God's pattern

✕ LESLIE ✕

As a Christian young woman navigating my way through the murky waters of the dating scene, I used to believe that God didn't have much interest in my love life other than to make sure I wasn't going too far. I had grown up in church, so I'd been subjected to many a "youth group purity pep talk" from the time I was eleven or twelve years old.

My parents made me read every popular book on the subject of Christian dating and go to every youth meeting at which the subject being addressed was "love, sex, and dating." So I was pretty confident that I knew God's thoughts on the subject of guy/girl relationships. All of the instruction I received from Christian voices could, in my opinion, be boiled down to two simple Christian dating rules:

Rule no. 1: Don't have sex until marriage.

Rule no. 2: Make sure you date only Christian guys who believe the same things you do about rule no. 1.

Even though I was raised in an upscale suburban neighborhood, attended a conservative church, and grew up in a loving Christian home, in the public school system I was exposed to the warped sexual climate of the culture from a young age. My peers started having oral sex in the bathrooms at school when they were twelve or thirteen. And by the time I got to high school, the majority of the girls I knew were hooking up with different guys every weekend, sleeping with guys they barely knew, and never expecting anything more than a one-night stand.

In this sex-saturated environment, following the two Christian dating rules seemed like a radical commitment.

My Not-So-Perfect Plan

I was sure God would be impressed if I graduated from high school a virgin. I figured the rest of my dating life was up to me. Somehow I perceived that as long as I obeyed those two Christian dating rules, I could pretty much make my own decisions regarding who to date, when to date, how to date, even who to get serious about. I truly desired to obey God and do things "the right way." But I was determined to create as much excitement as possible in my love life without compromising my Christian standards. If I wasn't hooking up with guy after guy like most of my friends, then at the very least I should be able to have *some* amount of fun in my dating life. I decided to go out with as many guys as I could, have as many boyfriends as possible, and experience every bit of pleasure I could without technically "crossing the line" and having sex before marriage.

Sure, someday I would meet the "right guy" and we would ride off into the sunset to live happily ever after. But as far as I was concerned, that was years away. It wouldn't happen until I was older and life had lost a little of its zest. And besides, I didn't think my high school dating relationships would have much impact on my relationship with my future husband. Surely he would understand that I was just trying to enjoy this season of my life, and he wouldn't hold anything over me. Especially if I saved my virginity until marriage.

So all throughout high school, I carelessly plunged into one temporary relationship after another, striving to maintain a string of boyfriends and going to all the dances, parties, and football games, where I would flirt, tease, and cavort with one guy after the next. Of course, if anything started to turn serious, I made sure it was with "Christian" guys who went to church. Typically, those guys weren't much different from any other sex-consumed, pornography-addicted guy at my school. But at least dating them *felt* more spiritual.

A few years went by, and I began to slowly awaken to the fact that, even though I'd set out to have fun and enjoy my high school years, I really wasn't happy. In fact, for the most part, I felt empty and depressed. On the outside it looked as though I was a solid, confident Christian young woman with a healthy dating life. I wasn't having sex with the guys I dated, and most of them were fairly moral guys who went to church and knew all the Sunday school stories by heart. My youth pastors would have applauded. But I felt distant from God. I began to realize that something was very out of place in my life.

Where I once had put my hope and confidence in my relationship with Christ, I now began to cling desperately to each relationship that came into my life as my source of security and purpose. My dating life became my identity. My emotions became hopelessly battered by each rocky relationship. The cutting, brutal pain of ending a relationship, no matter how serious or shallow it had been, drove me to constantly lower my "Christian" standards and bend the rules as much as possible, so as to somehow hold on to each guy who came into my life. I began to view purity as the edge of a cliff. "As long as I don't fall off the edge of the cliff, I'm fine," I would tell myself. I began to inch closer and closer to the precipice, giving more and more of my physical purity away, until I was teetering on the very brink of plummeting over. I told myself I was still pure, but in my heart of hearts, I knew better. With every step closer to the edge of that cliff, I had lost something precious. Maybe I wasn't sleeping with a new guy every weekend. But I was certainly giving my heart, mind, emotions, and body away to a series of guys.

I had dreamed of living a perfect fairy-tale love story someday. I had pictured a blissful and carefree dating life, just like what I watched on those old-fashioned black-and-white TV reruns. But I hadn't known about the ugly side of the temporary dating cycle: the inevitable heartbreak, confusion, and compromise of my spiritual values.

Brandon, the guy I wrote about earlier, was one of my more serious relationships. He was a popular basketball player I had managed to snag after meeting him at a game. Our casual, flirtatious friendship soon turned into a serious, passionate romance. I always felt so secure when Brandon put his arm gently on my shoulder as we entered a crowded room full of strangers.

The relationship went strong for about eight months, but then he started waking up to the fact that other girls were interested in him. And these other girls were more than willing to have sex with him.

Still attempting to follow Christian dating rule no. 1, I had told Brandon I couldn't sleep with him—even though I was willing to do just about everything short of that. At first, he had accepted this condition readily. He even said he agreed with my commitment to (technical) abstinence until marriage. But there came a point where I noticed his interested gaze resting upon other girls who looked at him seductively with open invitation. I could sense the end of our relationship coming. In desperation, I lowered my standards in the area of purity as much as I felt I possibly could, giving Brandon as many "physical favors" as I dared. But it was no use. Soon it was over, and he was giving his "love and devotion" to someone else, pretending he didn't even know who I was anymore. We had shared everything for almost a year of our lives, and now we were strangers.

This was the constant pattern of my life. Each fling ended with heartbreak and shattered emotions. Each time, I felt used and defiled. The perfect plan I had so carefully crafted for my dating career was crumbling. Before I even graduated from high school, I literally felt like I had been through the turmoil of about five divorces. I had no more confidence, no more security. I didn't know who I was anymore.

Giving God the Pen

It wasn't until I really started crying out to God in desperation that I awakened to the fact that I didn't have to live this way. For the first time I realized that God had more of an interest in my love life than just making sure I followed a few rules. He wanted to be involved. More than that, He wanted to write my love story for me…without my manipulative fingers constantly taking back the pen and trying to script it my way.

A mixture of emotions came with that realization. There was a glimmer of hope when I understood that the Author of romance actually wanted to write *my* love story. And yet the hope was instantly clouded by doubt and fear. Could God really do this without my brilliant input? Even though I had messed up my love life so far, I was pretty sure I still had *way more* insight into the finer things in life— like love, sex, dating, and marriage—than someone as old (and seemingly outdated) as God. What if He butchered the whole thing? I pictured myself trusting God with this precious area of my life, only to end up sitting in a long, gray, tentlike dress, staring forlornly out the window and rocking my life away in a rocking chair. No friends, no phone calls, no life whatsoever. I wouldn't get married until I was seventy-three, and it would be to some obnoxious guy I couldn't stand. We'd have four horrible years together, then die. That might sound extreme, but it was what I honestly feared would happen if I gave God the pen.

Tell God you are ready to be offered, and God will prove Himself to be all you ever dreamed He would be.[1]

OSWALD CHAMBERS

Looking back, I laugh at such a thought. That was before I learned what a true romantic God is. If I had only known what He had planned for me…I never would have doubted for a minute!

Even though I found it terrifying to entrust my romantic future to God, it was also a huge relief. I had been trying to make sense out of this area of my life for so long, and I had felt the pressure of figuring everything out for myself. *What if I marry the wrong person? What if I never meet the right guy? How will I know who the right one is? What if I make a mistake and ruin my whole life?* Worries like these had been my constant companions for years. Now God was inviting me to give all of these fears to Him—and to let Him lead and guide me through each step. I didn't have to carry the weight anymore; I could lay it completely in His hands. What freedom!

But was it too good to be true? Could I actually trust Him? Would He really take an active role in my love life? Would He lead and guide? And of even more concern to me was the question, would He lead me where I did *not* want to go? (The rocking chair scenario gave me nightmares!)

I went through several days of intense inner struggle. While the Christian world indicated that I was following God's way by keeping the dating rules, at least in a technical sense, I knew I was really doing things my own way. I had been the one calling the shots, not God.

Letting go of this area of my life seemed impossible. And yet a soft whisper to my heart reminded me that if I was ever going to be truly happy or fulfilled, and if I was ever going to stop making such a mess of things, *He* had to be at the center. Trusting Him completely with my love life was probably the hardest decision I had ever faced.

Finally, I surrendered to the gentle tug upon my heart. I knelt beside my bed and prayed, "Lord, it's so hard to give my love life to You. I desperately want to hold on to it and do things my way. Yet I know You are asking me to lay it in Your hands, to let You take charge of it. So, now, I give it to You. No matter what You choose to do with this area of my life, even if it's something I never would have chosen for myself, I give it to You. Do with me what You will. I am Yours."

My God-written love story began at that moment. God took the pen from my trembling hand and began scripting the most incredible tale imaginable. No, my future husband did not show up at my front door right then. But from that day on, God began healing and restoring the pain of my mistakes and molding and preparing me for *true* love. Before Eric came into my life, God had some important foundation stones to lay in place.

Priority Check

So I had given God the pen to write my love story. But practically, what did that mean for me on a daily basis? I was at the height of my "dating career" and not planning on marriage anytime soon. Was I supposed to stop dating? Were friendships with guys okay? How would I know when God *wanted* me to get into a relationship? When winking adults asked me that infamous question, "So, Leslie, is there any special guy in your life right now?" what was I supposed to say?

God was holding the pen and writing my story. What was *I* supposed to be doing?

During the weeks and months after my decision to allow God to control this area of my life, another gentle message was being communicated to my heart by His still, small whisper. It went something like this: *Leslie, don't try to build Me into your life anymore. Instead, build your life around Me.*

When I really stopped and looked at my life, I was startled to realize that I had tried to "fit God into my life" by praying each morning, reading my Bible every night, and attending church weekly. Yet He was not the central focus of my daily life. In reality I was only giving Him a few minutes of scattered attention here and there. I finally came to the realization that unless I slowed down and made a genuine effort to seek Him, instead of being so consumed with my own ambitions, I would have a hard time discerning His will for me in any area, especially my love life.

So I embarked on a journey to get to know my Creator. And truthfully, I wasn't sure what was going to happen. Up to this point, my life had revolved around a whirlwind of social activities, friends, and dating relationships, but now I was saying, "Lord, I'm going to lay all that aside and focus on You instead." Not that all of those things were necessarily wrong, but God was asking me to get my priorities straight. My dating and social life had become so distracting that I could no longer hear His voice clearly.

As Elisabeth Elliot says in her book *A Chance to Die* (about the life of Amy Carmichael), "The preoccupations of seventeen-year-old girls—their looks, their clothes, their social life—don't change much from generation to generation. But, in every generation there seem to be a few who make other choices. Amy Carmichael was one of the few."[2] God was calling me to be one of those "few" as well. But I didn't know how.

If You want this for me, Lord, You are going to have to help me, I told Him.

And He did. He met me right where I was and taught me about

Himself. I learned how to love Him with my whole heart, to seek Him earnestly, to listen to His voice on a daily basis, and to fall in love with His Word. It was the most exciting time of my life. It made my former world of social frenzy seem incredibly empty. Daily I discovered more about who He is and more about who He wanted me to become. I started a journal—and have kept it up to this very day—in which I wrote prayers, fears, and desires to the Lord. I also recorded anything I felt He might be teaching me, be it through Scripture or a gentle pull upon my heart. Now when I look back at my old entries, I am amazed at how faithful He was to put every detail of my life in place at the perfect time.

Yes, I lost some friends, but in reality they weren't true friends anyway. And yes, I lost popularity. I lost the constant attention and approval of guys. Yet what I gained was priceless: Jesus Christ as my first love, my most intimate heart-friend.

It may not seem that this part of my story has much to do with my relationship with Eric. But the change in my relationship with God was the whole key, for two reasons.

First, I learned to lean on my relationship with Christ for my hope, joy, and security, rather than trying to find those things in a romantic relationship. Eric is an incredible husband, but he is also human. If I had gone into my relationship with him looking for all my emotional needs to be met, I would have been disappointed. I wasn't truly ready to begin a journey toward marriage with my future husband until I learned to find my confidence, joy, and security first and foremost in Jesus Christ.

Second, Jesus Christ has always been at the center of my relation-

ship with Eric. Jesus Christ was the passion of my heart when I met Eric
Ludy. Jesus Christ was the passion of Eric's heart as well. As a result, we
were drawn together in friendship because of our mutual love for the
Lord. The more time we spent together, the closer we grew to God
through each other. Whenever I discovered a new truth in the Word of
God, I couldn't wait to share it with Eric. We spent hours talking about
our King and our faith. When our feelings for each other deepened
beyond friendship, God guided us each and every step as we began
moving into a romantic relationship, and He remained at the center.

In most Christian relationships, we are so caught up in our feelings for the other person that we unwittingly squeeze God into the
background. It becomes a confusing, emotional mess, and we wonder
why God isn't giving us more direction, when all the while He is there,
waiting to be allowed back into first place in our hearts. Only when
He is truly in first place are we ready for a God-written love story.

It's Not About a Formula

Even after you place your love life into the hands of God, it is so easy
to revert to looking for a "magic formula" to figure everything out. I
cannot count the number of times I get asked questions like, "Should
I date this person or not?" or "What do you do when you think you've
met the right one?"

To which I must reply, "Ask God."

People often get frustrated and say, "Well, I asked Him and He
isn't giving me any answers!"

Jana, a bubbly first-year student at a university in California, made the decision to give God the pen of her love story nearly two years ago. The problem is, since then Jana hasn't received any direction for this area of her life, and she is aggravated at God.

"I just don't get it," she complains. "When I gave this area to God, I expected Him to bring the right guy across my path. But every relationship I have gotten into has still turned out all wrong. Why isn't God getting involved? Why hasn't He done anything miraculous in this area of my life?"

As I look at Jana's daily life, I realize that although she attempted to give God control, she never reoriented her lifestyle to revolve around her relationship with Him. She expects answers from God without pursuing Him. Her idea of "seeking Him" is a once-a-week, five-minute Bible reading where she opens His Word randomly and reads whatever Scripture her eyes fall upon. No flash of divine wisdom comes, so she goes on her merry way, convinced that if God wants to speak to her, He'll send a heavenly messenger or a bolt of lightning to point her in the right direction.

The reason some of us are such poor specimens of Christianity is because we have no Almighty Christ. We have Christian attributes and experiences, but there is no abandonment to Jesus Christ.[3]

OSWALD CHAMBERS

Inviting God to write the chapters of our love story involves work on our part—not just a scattered prayer here and there, not merely a feeble attempt to find some insight by flopping open the Bible every now and then. It's seeking Him on a daily basis, putting Him in first place at all times, discovering His heart.

He may not come down with a bolt of lightning or paint a message for you in the sky, but as you truly get to know Him and His Word, you will understand His desires for you. It takes effort. It isn't easy. But it's the key to discovering the "sweeter song."

Wouldn't it be nice if we could write a book called *Ten Steps for Achieving a Perfect Love Story* and give you a foolproof, cookie-cutter blueprint for how it's all supposed to work?

But God cares too much about us to settle for a formula. He wants us to lean on Him for guidance and direction. He wants to be intimately involved in each detail, every step of the way. The minute we try to rely on a formula, we miss out on the whole beauty of what a God-written love story is all about. Eric and I have met plenty of people who are desperately trying to "get it right" by following a set of rules for a godly relationship. And they are usually miserable, frustrated, and depressed with the whole attempt.

Don't get me wrong. God gives us clear and unquestionable commands in Scripture for this area of our lives, such as sexual purity before marriage, avoiding marriage to an unbeliever, absolute faithfulness after marriage, etc. These guidelines come from a loving and faithful Father who wants us to experience love and romance in the beautiful, unhindered way He intended.

But there are a few gray areas that can leave us thoroughly confused. When it comes to the topic of relationships, the variety of opinions among Christians is endless.

The camp I grew up in put a heavy emphasis on keeping your technical virginity until marriage but fell short in presenting many other guidelines for building a God-honoring relationship. When it came to decisions about who to go out with and how much of your heart, mind, and body you should give that person, we were basically left to figure things out for ourselves.

At the opposite extreme is the camp that makes so many rules about relationships with the opposite sex that you have to tape a list to your bathroom mirror to remember them all.

And of course there is every teaching in between these two extremes. The problem is that no matter what side of the pendulum swing we are on—just doing the bare minimum requirement or going to ultrastrict extremes—if we are trying to follow a rule just because we have to, inside we become resentful and begrudging. We aren't obeying commands because we love God and want to please Him; we are doing it simply because it's expected of us.

Relationship Rules

Trying to build a foolproof formula for a godly relationship can only end in failure. Whenever we rely solely on rules to protect us, we push God out of first place in our lives.

As I said, I grew up with the "just-don't-have-sex-before-marriage" mentality, thinking that as long as I gave it a shot and attempted to keep from falling off the edge of the cliff (in other words, not technically having sex before marriage), this area of my life would be protected from harm. However, the boundaries I created for myself still gave me plenty of room to compromise. Even though I had not officially "overstepped" the lines I had drawn, I was living a life of heartache and despair.

Sarah, a spunky college senior, had an experience at the other extreme. She came from a church with excessively strict and specific rules about guy/girl relationships.

Sarah met John, the resident "godly-hot-guy-with-cute-curls" at church, and eventually they felt God leading them toward marriage. They followed every rule down to the last letter. From the outside, it would appear as if there was no way they could fall into any sort of compromise with such strict supervision and guidelines. They were never allowed to be alone together; they weren't even permitted to have any sort of physical contact; and their parents were intimately involved in every decision about their relationship.

Sarah recalls, "We were so confident that we were following the right path, we thought we were immune to sin."

But rules did not save them from temptation, and one day Sarah and John broke all the rules and stumbled into sexual sin. Sarah became pregnant. This couple disappointed their families, their church, and themselves, but they learned a valuable lesson: no matter how many rules we make for ourselves, rules don't create a godly relationship. Only leaning on God alone and allowing Him to guide and direct every part of our existence will set the stage for a beautiful romance!

Is It a Chore or a Choice?

When I was eight, my parents forced me into slave labor; they made me clean up the kitchen every night after dinner. I wasn't too thrilled about such a chore, and I made sure to let them know it. "You treat me just like Cinderella!" I accused them, while dramatically leaning on the broom with a beaten and downtrodden look, as if I were going to faint from exhaustion. (My pathetic cry for mercy never seemed to move my parents to sympathy.)

But no matter how much I despised cleaning up the kitchen, I always did it anyway. Why? Because I knew that negative consequences would result if I didn't. My parents made terrible threats, like grounding me from my bike or sending me to my room if I didn't obey. I did the bare minimum requirement just to get the job done, and I constantly asked, "Can I be done yet?!" until they finally set me free from the dungeon of kitchen-torture.

Of course, there were occasional exceptions to this forced-labor scenario. We all had our angelic moments as children. For me, those moments were rare, but still they did exist. I can remember one evening when my parents went out for the night. The kitchen was a mess, but no one asked me to clean it. I got the brilliant idea to do something special for Mom and Dad. So I set to work, all by myself, and scrubbed the dishes. I did an extra-careful job to get them sparkling clean. I even wiped up the counters and swept the floor. I couldn't wait for my parents to come home and notice what I'd done. When they arrived and exclaimed, "Who cleaned up the kitchen? This is wonderful!" my heart swelled with pride. I actually *enjoyed* the whole process. Cleaning the kitchen went from a dull

In our abandonment we give ourselves over to God just as God gave Himself for us, without any calculation. The consequences of abandonment never enter into our outlook because our life is taken up with Him.[4]

OSWALD CHAMBERS

drudgery to an act of joy. Why? Because I was motivated not by a rule but by love for my parents.

When obeying God is a chore we are forced to do, it becomes a lifeless act of drudgery and we complain the whole way through. God becomes the Big-No-Fun-One who is trying to make our lives miserable.

But when we learn who God *really* is and we base our decisions on a passionate love for Him, we find joy and delight in obedience. We even *want* to go that extra mile for Him.

What It's Really All About

As Christians, we need a new mind-set toward God's involvement in this area of our lives. Whether you grew up with the "just-try-not-to-have-premarital-sex" crowd or you had a ten-page rulebook for relationships, either approach denies the beauty of God's ways.

Remember the infamous question that popped up so often back in the days of youth-group powwow sessions: *How far is too far?* This question is really a code for asking, "How much can I get away with and not make God mad?" It's not even a question a devoted follower of Christ should be asking in the first place.

Rather, we should be motivated by an entirely different question: "How far can I possibly go to bring joy to the heart of my heavenly Father in this area of my life?"

Once you get to know your King in a personal way, once Jesus Christ becomes the focus and passion of your life, it's not hard at all to ask that question, because it flows from a heart of overwhelming love for your Lord. If you say genuinely, "How can I please you, Lord?"

He will show you, each and every day, in His own gentle way. The answer won't be drudgery to which you are forced to comply. When you love Him, *really* love Him, you will be able to say with David the psalmist, "I *delight* to do Your will, O my God" (Psalm 40:8, emphasis added).

God has created us all as individuals, and He has a unique and special plan for each of our lives. *Don't settle for a formula.* If you're ready for an unforgettable earthly romance, start by discovering the joy of an intimate, daily romance with the King of kings. When you truly know Him like that, you'll never again ask the question, "How far is too far?"

For what the law could not do in that it was weak through the flesh, God did by sending His own Son.

ROMANS 8:3

How much more shall the blood of Christ…cleanse your conscience from dead works to serve the living God?

HEBREWS 9:14

I will instruct you and teach you in the way you should go.

PSALM 32:8

A Look Inside Your Heart

1. In what ways have you "pre-scripted" the way you think your love story should unfold? What specifically would change in your life if you yielded to God's perfect plan for this area rather than pursuing your own agenda?

2. What relationship failures have you endured in the past? What misplaced expectations, if any, can you identify that may have contributed to those failures?

3. What "magic formulas" have you used in the past to navigate the gray areas of relationships? How well did those formulas work?

4. In what ways would your approach to relationships change if you focused not on rules or formulas but on asking the question, "How can I please you, Lord?"

A Step Further

There's no time like the present to prayerfully examine your heart. Are your decisions in this area of your life motivated by rules, or by a relationship? Are you following God's prescription out of duty and obligation, or out of genuine love for your King? Are you allowing Christ intimate access to this area of your life, or are you keeping Him at arm's length? We encourage you to ask God's Spirit to reveal any selfish attitudes or patterns in your life, and by His grace, determine to walk a different way.

Part Two

The Art
of Faithfulness

Loving Your Spouse Even Before You Ever Meet

Five

Get a Love Life

What faithfulness really looks like

ERIC

"Hey, Eric!" Steve boomed as I was getting comfortable in the yellow plastic McDonald's booth. "Bob's picking the Huskers to beat your Buffs by twenty!"

"What?" I bellowed. "Bob, your Huskers will be lucky to come out of Folsom Field *alive,* let alone with a victory!"

Ah...those memorable college days. There I was with my buddies who, like me, were once again dateless on yet another Friday night. To soothe our egos, we had headed to the place so near and dear to all of us—McDonald's—to splurge our carefully budgeted spare ninety-nine cents on a sumptuous chocolate-vanilla swirl cone and engage in some serious guy talk.

If you're a female reader who is interested in discovering how guys tick, just listen up. Whenever college guys huddle together in a plastic yellow booth, they become very predictable, at least in their conversation.

First they talk about sports. They argue, bellow, sweat, flex, and all sorts of tough things like that. Once they exhaust that topic, they start talking about another favorite subject: food. More specifically, *cheap* food.

"Did you know that Zip's is selling five cheeseburgers for two bucks now?"

"Dude, I just bought twenty Top Ramens for two bucks at Rosauers!"

Eventually they cover all the important bases regarding their digestive system, and move on to their endocrine system, where all their hormones hang out.

This Friday night conversation was no different. I think it happened at precisely the same moment that Bob excitedly told us the news about the "gorgeous blonde" from Sweeney Hall who was proofreading his paper on "Ducks and Deadly Diseases." I felt a little knock on my heart.

Clank, clank!

It was God, reminding me of His position in this ever-so-important area of my life. It had been a few months since I "let go of my pen," and still, at times, I was struggling with trusting Him.

Clank, clank!

I had experienced some moments of serious doubt as to the reliability of God in the area of romance. But as He again knocked this fateful Friday night, I was reminded of not only the fact that I had entrusted Him with the pen of my love life, but that He had given me a little something too. He had given me *a beautiful hope.* It was a hope that He was preparing a special someone to perfectly match my life. But I had to trust Him.

Clank, clank!

I remember drifting off into la-la land as Bob shared how his "gorgeous blonde" gently touched his hand after she found a grammatical error in the opening line of his "Ducks and Deadly Diseases" essay. I was physically present with my college buddies at that plastic table, but my mind had taken a radical detour. For the first time in my life, I was beginning to realize that if God's plan and purpose for my life really was marriage, then the person I was going to one day marry was most likely *somewhere* on this great big planet. And right at that moment she was doing *something*. I was swallowed up in one gigantic thought: *She's alive.*

Have you ever thought about that? Just ponder it for a moment. If God's plan and purpose for you is marriage, then the person you will one day marry (unless he or she is not born yet) is alive and wandering the earth. If that's true, if your future love really is out there somewhere, don't you wonder what that person is doing right now?

That's precisely what I thought. *I wonder what she's doing tonight.*

I pondered the fact that it was a Friday night and that there was a full moon in the sky. I wondered if she was looking at the same moon I was and maybe even thinking of me. Everything was lovely. Then it hit me.

What if she's with another guy right now?

My mind was filled with a grotesque image of a sleazy, smirking hulk, slinking his arm, snakelike, around my future wife's shoulder.

Then, when I didn't think it could get any worse, I imagined this sweet-talking imposter pulling my wife close…and kissing her.

At this thought, my face twisted into a snarl, and my eyes narrowed with indignation. My right hand formed a pulsating fist and smacked my open left hand with savage force. I was ready to *kill* this guy! He was touching something that was solely mine!

I'm glad there wasn't a video camera on me as I sat there in that plastic booth. My buddies and I never talked about it afterward (believe me, I didn't dare bring it up). Maybe they thought my little tirade was an allergic reaction to ice cream cone dust or something. But on a night where I blew a whopping ninety-nine cents on something I enjoyed for only five and a half minutes, I also gained an invaluable little truth I will enjoy for the rest of my life.

As this disturbing picture of my future wife and the imposter filled my head, God *clank, clanked* upon my heart. It was almost as if His great big fatherly arm wrapped itself around my shoulder. In a way only God can, He nudged my heart and slipped me a little note.

"Eric," this imaginary note read, "you desire purity in your wife, don't you?"

"You'd better believe I do!" I trumpeted in response. "I want my wife to be *pure!*"

"That's great, Eric," the note continued. "I'm glad you're interested in purity. I'm quite a fan of it Myself."

It was then that I learned the life lesson.

"But just think, Eric. If you desire purity in your wife, how much more do you think she desires purity...*in you?*"

The Donny Lucero Effect

I guess it happened somewhere in junior high, between a Donny Lucero lecture on the "looseness" of girls and an informal discussion

I overheard among the cheerleaders about how someone needed to invent a female condom so that girls could have more control in a sexual relationship. I finally just came to the decision that there wasn't a girl in the whole wide world who was going to set herself aside for me in real purity.

We can call it the "Donny Lucero effect." Our desire for something beautiful is strong at first. We long, we believe, and we even wait for this "something beautiful," sort of like we believe in the Tooth Fairy and Santa. But we all have our moments when we grasp "reality." We gradually realize that we never see it, we never hear of it, and we never sniff even the slightest scent that this "something beautiful" even exists. Then there comes a moment in our lives when Donny Lucero's words are that last piece of straw that finally breaks the backbone of our once-confident desire.

"That's it!" we mutter in exasperation. "I'm not going to save something for someone who's not saving something for me!"

The Donny Lucero effect got me, and I wouldn't be surprised to learn that it's gotten you too. I mean, why would I go to all the trouble of denying my desires for so many years if the person I'm doing it for isn't doing the same for me? What a waste!

I pondered my love life as I sat in that plastic booth that memorable Friday night. I pondered what it meant to truly love someone and what it meant to be pure.

For years I had wanted the world around me to think I was "the sex machine." Here I was a virgin, but I wanted people to think I wasn't. If you had set both Jesus Christ and wormy little Donny Lucero in front of me and said, "Eric, we'll give you a choice. You can be shaped into the likeness and share the same nature with either the King of the universe or with this sex-crazed jerk over here named Donny. Which would you prefer? Consider wisely, Eric, because you'll have to live with your decision."

It is humbling for me to admit, but up until this point in my life, I would have probably chosen the sex-crazed jerk over Jesus. Donny's life seemed so appealing on the outside. It seemed his every desire was met, his every craving thoroughly enjoyed. What I didn't take into account was his empty and purposeless life, endlessly searching for meaning, acceptance, and love.

Purity Is a Sweeter Song

With God tenderly standing by my side, I finished reading the little note He had slipped me. The last line read, "It is more blessed to give, Eric, than to receive" (see Acts 20:35).

It was Orpheus's "sweeter song" all over again. That word *blessed*—that same word that illuminates the way to supreme happiness. It was found in thinking about what I could *give* instead of what I could *get*.

For my entire life, I had wanted my future spouse to do me the favor of staying pure, giving me a little respect, and proving to me that I was the love of her life. I was hungering for the beautiful side of love, but I never realized that I would find it when I started to focus on the way I lived and loved and not on the way she lived and loved. And that I would find it when I finally focused on honoring her *before we met*, even if she never considered honoring me in return.

My invaluable ninety-nine-cent lesson was this: Eric, do you really want that sweeter song? Then set your life aside as a priceless treasure, kept polished and pure, for your future spouse. When she one day receives that gift, there won't be a love song in all the earth that can express the beauty and romance of such a moment. Only heaven could play a melody sweet enough!

That very scenario was played out two thousand years ago by a Bridegroom named Jesus for His Bride. The universe has never been the same.

Eyes for Only One

"I'm just reading the articles!"

Ah, yes! The famous quote never to be forgotten throughout the history of McDuffey Hall. Spoken like a true guy when he was brought before the self-appointed college morality board with a *Playboy* magazine in hand. The rest of the quote went something like, "Don't worry, I'm not even looking at the pictures!"

Well, every guy who has ever salivated over baby back ribs on an empty stomach can join me in saying, "Yeah, right!"

Purity goes more than skin deep. There isn't an honest man alive who would deny it.

Your entire body—everything from your heart to your mind to the skin that holds it

Do all things without complaining and disputing, that you may become blameless and harmless, children of God without fault in the midst of a crooked and perverse generation, among whom you shine as lights in the world.

PHILIPPIANS 2:14–15

all in place—is a treasure. Yet for some reason, our generation of Christians only views purity as an external thing; as long as we're not having sex, we are supposedly pure.

Imagine that God wants to bring into your life someday a remarkable guy or girl who will make your heart skip a beat every time you look their way.

Imagine that this future spouse of yours can see you right now. Pretend that he or she is capable of watching you, *everywhere* you go, and able to see *everything* you do and hear *everything* you say.

Then ask yourself this question: *If my future spouse followed me around throughout my day, every day of my life, would he or she feel cherished and adored by me as I interact with the opposite sex? Would he or she feel loved by my actions or feel hurt that I am giving away what belongs to only my future spouse?*

For instance, what if I had been spending that Friday night with a pretty blonde instead of with my dateless buddies? What if my future wife could see me slithering *my* snakelike arm around another girl's shoulder? What if she could witness me kissing someone else? Do you think she would be cheering me on?

I don't think so. In fact, I know exactly how Leslie would respond to such a scene. She would have wet eyes and a crushed heart because I was giving my love and affection to someone other than her.

Marriage vows are a heavy-duty thing. In front of a whole crowd of witnesses you are announcing your love and your lifelong faithfulness to your spouse. Whether in sickness or in health, makeup on or makeup off, *you're committed.* Many of us wait until the very last possible moment to be committed to the man or woman we will spend the rest of life with. That's sort of like not ever touching a basketball in your life and then trying out for the Harlem Globetrotters. You'll shoot a lot of air balls that way. The secret to amazing romance is to begin practicing purity for your spouse and cherishing that person with your thoughts, actions, and words *long* before you even meet him or her.

It became my goal, from the night I blew my whopping ninety-nine cents at McDonald's, to live as if my future wife could see me. I wanted to adore her and cherish her before I even met her. And I realized I could do that by choosing, in every situation life brought my way, to think of her as if she were right beside me and to consider how my decisions would affect her.

Six months before our wedding, Leslie told me, "Eric, I wish you had never had a desire for another girl in your entire life."

Whether or not that is an unrealistic request for a woman to have is beside the point. The point is this: the *desire* she had (and your future spouse has right now, even though you may not yet have met) is that

When I am around the other men and they talk about anything remotely immoral, I don't join in. Rather, I confront them head-on and tell them they are wrong to talk about women that way. Also, I wear a purity ring, which brings me a lot of bewilderment from other young men my age who have already thrown away their purity. But I don't care how other people respond, because it reminds me what I'm waiting for.

PADDEN, AGE 21

you would be a "one-woman man" or a "one-man woman" your entire life, not just after you two connect.

Whether or not your future spouse remains faithful to you is beside the point. Christ gave Himself willingly for us, His Bride, even when we had gone astray and turned to other lovers. If you love your spouse the way He loves you, you'll set the stage for a marriage that rivals the greatest love stories of all time.

I can't encourage you strongly enough to give your future spouse your heart, mind, and body now. It's easy to run from one shallow relationship to the next, meeting your own selfish desires. But it takes a real man to keep one woman satisfied for life, and it takes a real woman to keep a man's heart captivated for life. I guarantee you, the rewards of real faithfulness are off-the-charts amazing.

Suppressing Sexuality?

The other day Leslie and I were speaking to a group of Bible college students about the sacredness of sex and God's marvelous design for making a marriage beautiful. A skeptical girl in the front row piped up.

"Are you saying that we are supposed to just suppress our sexuality until we get married?" The tone of her voice sent one very clear message: *that's totally unrealistic.*

The general consensus among these students seemed to be that lust, pornography, masturbation, and sexual compromise are an inseparable part of being young and single. Some of them, like Leslie and me, had tried to maintain their technical virginity prior to marriage in order to stay in God's good graces. But nearly all of them were enslaved to some kind of sexual vice and didn't seem to think it was necessary, or even possible, to live differently.

I remember having similar thoughts early in my college days. *Maybe I should just have sex now and ask my wife's forgiveness later,* I would reason whenever a cute girl flashed me an inviting look. *I'm sure she'll understand that I'm a guy and I'm just built this way. What's so important about purity, anyway?*

What's the Big Deal About Purity?

In recent years, many Christians have become more and more lax about truth as certain voices have emerged onto the scene challenging us to rethink our entire approach toward God and His Word. "We're not supposed to take the Bible *literally,*" is one frequent message. "We're just supposed to interpret it in a way that actually works in our modern culture."

When we start reasoning this way, we stop taking God at His Word. Things that have always been part of God's prescription and design, like purity, start to seem unrealistic and unimportant. In a world where it's not uncommon for twelve-year-olds to have oral sex in the bathrooms at school or for high-schoolers to engage in every conceivable kind of sexual act with multiple partners at a time, it can be tempting to redefine God's standard of purity to align with the reality of modern culture. A little harmless flirting or touching, a bit of pornography or lustful fantasies, and even a bit of sexual compromise here and there hardly seems like a big deal compared with the way the rest of the world is living.

But when was the last time we really got in touch with how God feels about sexual compromise? If we choose to actually take His Word at face value, we come face to face with the fact that purity is not something He takes lightly:

Flee sexual immorality. Every sin that a man does is outside the body, but he who commits sexual immorality sins against his own body. Or do you not know that your body is the temple of the Holy Spirit who is in you, whom you have from God, and you are not your own? For you were bought at a price; therefore glorify God in your body and in your spirit, which are God's. (1 Corinthians 6:18–20)

Do you not know that the unrighteous will not inherit the kingdom of God? Do not be deceived. Neither fornicators, nor idolaters, nor adulterers, nor homosexuals, nor sodomites…will inherit the kingdom of God. (1 Corinthians 6:9–10)

You have heard that it was said to those of old, "You shall not commit adultery." But I say to you that whoever looks at a woman to lust for her has already committed adultery with her in his heart. If your right eye causes you to sin, pluck it out and cast it from you; for it is more profitable for you that one of your members perish, than for your whole body to be cast into hell. And if your right hand causes you to sin, cut it off and cast it from you; for it is more profitable for you that one of your members perish, than for your whole body to be cast into hell. (Matthew 5:27–30)

If my heart has been enticed by a woman, or if I have lurked
at my neighbor's door…that would be wickedness; yes, it
would be iniquity deserving of judgment. For that would be
a fire that consumes to destruction, and would root out all
my increase. (Job 31:9–12)

I realize these are not popular Scriptures to bring up. In fact, at first
glance they probably seem more along the lines of "thou shalt nots"
than the beautiful sweeter song. Many of us grew up with a version of
Christianity that hammered us over the head with rules yet never
acquainted us with God's true heart. The "thou shalt nots" were not
described as loving boundaries from a faithful Father who loves us more
than we can comprehend and knows how we can enjoy His very best
for our lives. Rather, they were communicated as stern, angry commands from an unfeeling Being who's determined to make us miserable.

Several generations back, Christianity in this country began to
swing in an unhealthy direction, focusing on the holiness and righteous standard of God while excluding the crucial elements of love and
grace. Christians tried to live uprightly in their own strength, without
the enabling power of the Spirit of God. The result was a stiff religious
legalism that pushed people away from the faith in droves.

Today, many have swung to the opposite extreme. Trying to balance the unloving, super-religious hypocrisy of past generations and
redeem the bad reputation it gave to Christianity, a large number of
modern pastors and Christian leaders have overemphasized the unconditional love and forgiveness of God. As a result, quite a few key
elements of the true Christian life, such as holiness, righteousness, and
purity have become taboo subjects in many churches.

A young Christian couple Leslie and I knew quite well fell into sexual sin several months before their wedding. The response from their Christian parents, their pastor, and most of their Christians friends was the same: *it's really not that big of a deal.* Anyone who expressed concern about the fact that they were living in ongoing sexual compromise was labeled a legalistic extremist who was taking the Word of God far too seriously. Sadly, this mentality is becoming quite common. The general attitude of more and more modern Christians goes something like this: *Sure, purity before marriage is fine if you can do it, but most people can't. And we really shouldn't make that big a deal out of it; God loves us all the same, whether we're pure or not.*

But we cannot separate purity and holiness from the Christian life. God is love, but He is also holy. It is impossible for us to walk in darkness and light simultaneously. We cannot serve both sin and the kingdom of God at the same time. We cannot live a life of impurity and remain in unhindered fellowship with the King of kings.

The Pattern for Beautiful Romance

God has set up a clear pattern for beautiful romance. We cannot experience the kind of love, sex, and intimacy we long for unless we follow His pattern. And His pattern is purity. Following His pattern means living in absolute faithfulness—body, mind, and heart—to one person for a lifetime. It means honoring God's marriage covenant as sacred, saving every expression of sexual intimacy for *after* the covenant wedding vows are spoken. It means treating sexuality not as an opportunity to gratify selfish desires, but as an opportunity to selflessly serve our spouse.

When a husband daily lays down his life for his wife, considers her needs above his own, and sacrifices his own agenda in order to be sensitive to her, he will truly become the man that she desires above any other. When a wife builds her existence around serving her husband, meeting his needs, and thinking of his good above her own, her man will respond with a radical adoration for her alone. It's a pattern that begins long before the wedding day by...laying down our own selfish wants and honoring God's context for sex.[1]

ERIC LUDY, *MEET MR. SMITH*

Following God's prescription for purity is what leads to the sweeter song. When we comprehend the fact that God designed purity not to hinder us or make us miserable, but to protect us from heartache and to free us to experience His highest and best, we finally start to realize why purity is so important in God's plan. He asks us to embrace purity because He loves us desperately and wants us to experience the incredible fullness and beauty He intended for romance.

Sexuality is like fire. When kept in its rightful place, a fire adds the beauty of warmth and light to a home. But if fire escapes its proper context, it can burn down the entire house in a matter of minutes. Our God cares about us far too much to allow our lives to be destroyed by sexuality. So He asks us to keep it in its proper context. Then and only then can it be the beautiful, fulfilling gift He created it to be.

This is not to say that all hope is lost if you have already given away your purity. On the contrary, the entire reason Christ came to this earth and died was to give us freedom from our sins—a fresh start, a clean slate, and a new beginning. (We'll talk more about this in chapter 14.)

Living a life of inward and outward purity in today's lust-driven, sex-crazed world can seem next to impossible. Guys are under extreme pressure to prove they are sexual players. Girls feel the need to prove they are anything but prudes. But the incredible thing about God's commands is that He doesn't leave us to fulfill them in our own lim-

> *His divine power has given to us all things that pertain to life and godliness.*
>
> 2 PETER 1:3

ited, feeble strength. Rather, when we surrender our lives fully and completely to Him, He provides everything we need to live the life of purity He's called us to.

Contrary to that young college student's assumption, purity doesn't mean suppressing sexuality prior to marriage. Living in real purity means allowing the Spirit of God to overtake your life to the point where you are no longer living to feed the selfish cravings of your flesh. It means being far more consumed with honoring God and your future spouse than with fulfilling the demands of your selfish desires. Paul tells us that if we walk in the Spirit, we will not fulfill the lust of the flesh (Galatians 5:16).

Purity is not merely the absence of sexual indulgence, but the presence of God's Spirit in every dimension of our life. In the true Christian life, we are to be so caught up in our relationship with Christ that we no longer live to serve ourselves, but Him. When that happens, our desires become His desires. We actually begin to *value* and *love* the things that He values and loves, like purity. And we aren't walking around trying to suppress our sexuality; rather, purity naturally flows from our life. It becomes our joy and privilege to live in a way that honors God and our future spouse. Purity of the mind and body is a natural outflow of a pure, cleansed, Christ-consumed heart.

Putting Sex in Its Rightful Place

I once heard about a woman who lived out in the country and was frequently visited by a large brown bear who would scavenge her trash bin for food. The woman thought the bear was kind of cute, so she started leaving food out for him. When the bear caught wind of the fact that this was a place to get free food, he came back—and brought his friends. Pretty soon the bears were tearing up the landscaping, breaking down fences, and even threatening to break down the door of the house in order to get more food.

Although she found their out-of-control behavior stressful and even frightening, for some reason the woman kept feeding the bears. An animal lover at heart, she felt obligated to continue feeding them now that they seemed so dependent upon her as a food source. After all, she didn't want them to starve! The bears continued to wreak havoc on the woman's property, driving her to the point of insanity, until she finally sought advice from a forest ranger. The ranger's prescription was simple. "If you want to get rid of the bears," he told her, "stop feeding them."

Sexuality is a lot like those wild bears. Once we start feeding our sexual desires, they get stronger and more aggressive. They bring their friends. They begin to take control of us and wreak havoc upon our lives. We feel helpless against their power. But the solution is far simpler than you might think: *stop feeding them.*

Sensuality is everywhere in our culture, from sex-filled movies to seductive magazine covers. It's all too easy to buy into the propaganda right along with the rest of the world and continually feed the lustful cravings of our sexual longings—whether by toying with a little Internet porn, or watching movies filled with nudity and sex scenes, or allowing our own minds to run rampant with sexual fantasies. Technically, we're not having sex, but we've allowed our minds and even our bodies to feed on lust and impurity.

To be a one-woman man or a one-man woman doesn't mean simply guarding your heart, mind, and body when you're interacting with the opposite sex; it means guarding your heart, mind, and body *all* the time. Imagine that your future spouse could observe your innermost thoughts, watch what you view on the Internet, and see which movies you watch. If you are allowing sexual desires to control you, chances are you're not making decisions that honor your future spouse, whether or not you technically remain a virgin.

Abide in Me, and I in you. As the branch cannot bear fruit of itself, unless it abides in the vine, neither can you, unless you abide in Me. I am the vine, you are the branches. He who abides in Me, and I in him, bears much fruit; for without Me you can do nothing.

JOHN 15:4–5

So take the forest ranger's advice: stop feeding them. As Peter says, "…not conforming yourselves to the former lusts, as in your ignorance; but as He who called you is holy, you also be holy in all your conduct" (1 Peter 1:14–15).

Ask God's Spirit to show you how to stop feeding your lustful desires. This may require some difficult decisions, like cutting out certain movies, setting up accountability for the Internet, and training your mind to dwell on heavenly things rather than sensual things throughout the day (and as you fall asleep at night). But again, it's not something God asks you to do in your own willpower. He has promised to give you His divine power to help you live a godly life. The more you cultivate your relationship with Him, the more you'll begin to feel His incredible strength giving you the kind of victory you could never win on your own.

But What If...?

One enormous question still hangs in the air.

"What if I *don't* get married?"

That's a fair question. I mean, it's one thing to set aside all of those desires if they one day will be satisfied in marriage, but what if they *never* are? What if it isn't God's intention for you to ever take wedding vows? Why would what you do now matter if no future spouse will be affected by your decisions?

One of the richest and most priceless things we can learn is this simple truth: Even if we *never* get married, *nothing* we do in guarding our hearts, filtering our thoughts, and cherishing our future spouse by the way we live will be wasted. It is not merely for our future marriage here on earth that we do these things; it is also an investment in our glorious future marriage in heaven with Jesus.

Far more important than what our future spouse thinks or feels is what our King thinks and feels. Does He feel sorrowful as He watches our lives? Or does He feel honored and adored by the way we are living?

Even though it's absolutely true that following God's ways leads to life, beauty, and fulfillment, personal reward should never be our motivation for following His perfect design. We are to give everything to Him because He gave everything for us. We are to gladly love and serve Him with every breath we take because *He is worthy.* This life is not about us; it's about Him.

For most of my life I followed in the footsteps of Donny Lucero instead of Christ. I thank Jesus that He was patient with me and didn't base His commitment to me on my loyalty to Him. I'm certain on many days His eyes were wet with tears shed over my reckless ways. But I'm with Him now, listening to a sweeter song, learning to love Leslie the way He first loved me. And I wouldn't trade ten million difficult footsteps of following Christ for even one sleazy little shuffle of Donny Lucero's feet.

And this I pray, that your love may abound still more and more in knowledge and all discernment, that you may approve the things that are excellent, that you may be sincere and without offense till the day of Christ, being filled with the fruits of righteousness which are by Jesus Christ, to the glory and praise of God.

PHILIPPIANS 1:9–11

Let nothing be done through selfish ambition or conceit, but in lowliness of mind let each esteem others better than himself. Let each of you look out not only for his own interests, but also for the interests of others. Let this mind be in you which was also in Christ Jesus, who, being in the form of God, did not consider it robbery to be equal with God, but made Himself of no reputation, taking the form of a bondservant.

PHILIPPIANS 2:3–7

A Look Inside Your Heart

1. What are some ways you hope your future spouse is being faithful to you now, before you ever meet?
2. If your future spouse could see your interactions with the opposite sex, or even read your thoughts, would he or she feel loved and cherished or hurt and jealous? Explain your answer.
3. What changes in behavior would help you stop fueling sexual temptation in your life?
4. In what specific ways can you begin to love and cherish your future spouse right now?

A Step Further

Writing a love letter to your future spouse is one of the best ways to solidify your commitment to the one you'll spend your life with. This exercise also will help you realize that your future spouse is real, not just a theoretical concept. While I was waiting for God to bring Leslie into my life, I endured many nights of loneliness and many days of great impatience. Writing her love letters in those times reminded me of my commitment to her and affirmed that my future love story was truly worth waiting for. ✳

Six

A Forever Kind of Love

Romance that's more than a feeling

✖ LESLIE ✖

Have you ever been so deliriously in love with someone that you turned into a crazy person? When Eric and I were engaged, we were idiotically in love. We were separated by twelve hundred miles for most of that six-month period, and I am so glad no one recorded our phone conversations. We had a gushy, sappy, ridiculous love language that sounded almost like baby talk. Those days are nothing short of embarrassing to recall.

One time while Eric was on a trip, he was staying at a house with a buddy named Ryan (a single guy who had no appreciation for what it means to be idiotically in love). Late one night as soon as Eric thought the coast was clear, he sneaked away to call me. As he poured out his heart to me in his classic lovey-dovey voice (which sounded a bit like Winnie the Pooh on helium), Ryan was behind the wall eavesdropping and dying with laughter. He would have paid a fortune for a recording device.

When we think of being in love with someone, usually passion is what comes to mind—those overwhelming feelings of adoration and devotion, not to mention intense physical attraction. We often base our feelings for another person on what our hormones tell us. When we are physically attracted to someone, every time that person walks into the room, our fire is lit and we start reasoning from sexual desire rather than from common sense.

Let's face it: attraction is fun. And where would any relationship be without an element of that brain-liquefying kind of passion? But here is a critical question: is passion strong enough to build a lasting love upon?

Happily Ever After?

In case you haven't noticed yet, emotion-based love tends to be fairly unstable. One minute you can be so madly in love with someone you can't imagine life without them, and the next day you wonder what you ever saw in them at all. Most of my dating relationships were nothing more than a roller-coaster ride of emotions—the high points were when the passion was at its peak; the low points were when those feelings started to fade.

Another unstable factor is the element of physical beauty. Beauty inevitably fades with time. When did you last see a group of young men out on a Friday night turn their heads when a ninety-seven-year-old woman hobbled by on a walker? She's not likely to hear catcalls and shouts of "Hey baby!" from these potent young males! Beauty does *not* last forever.

This used to worry me when I contemplated marriage. *If passion comes and goes, and physical beauty fades with time, how do I know our love will last?*

And those concerns in this day and age are quite valid. Who would ever dream of falling head over heels in love, riding off into the sunset toward happily ever after...and then getting divorced? Yet for too many couples, that fairy-tale-turned-nightmare hits all too close to home. Divorce is sweeping our culture in epidemic proportions.

In fact, studies show the divorce rate among Christians has now *surpassed* non-Christians! Pollster George Barna recently released a study that shows those describing themselves as born-again Christians actually have a higher divorce rate than do those who claim no belief in Jesus Christ.[1]

As you look ahead toward marriage someday, how can you keep from becoming one more statistic? How can you know your love story will last a lifetime?

The answer lies in the *kind* of love upon which you choose to build your relationship. If you build it purely on emotion or sexual desire, you most certainly *are* headed for divorce, because one day you'll wake up and realize those feelings aren't there anymore.

Someone once told me, "Dating is great preparation for marriage. By dating around, you learn what you want in a marriage partner." As much as I liked that statement at the time, I soon realized that dating around *wasn't* preparing me very well for marriage. In fact, if I were to be honest, it was setting me up better for divorce. On a whim, I would dive headfirst into a relationship, let things quickly become emotionally and physically intense, and then when those feelings faded, I'd go out and find someone new—a constant cycle of *temporary* relationships. But God didn't intend for marriage to be temporary. And by living this way, I wasn't preparing to love one man for a lifetime; I was preparing to have multiple short-lived, emotion-based romantic flings.

Temporary Flings Equal Permanent Damage

I found out quickly that my dating life was not going to be the blissful experience I had imagined it would be. No one prepared me for the emotional pain involved in this lifestyle. Every time a relationship ended, it felt like someone had reached inside my chest and ripped my heart out, then shattered it on the ground into a million pieces. I had never known such pain.

And thus began the vicious cycle. Each time a relationship ended, whether it had been serious or casual, long-term or only two weeks long, I felt crushed emotionally and went on a desperate search for another boyfriend.

Dating became like an addictive drug to me: I used relationships to help me feel confident and secure in life. If I was ever *without* a guy, I became agitated, restless, and insecure. So I made sure those times were rare.

The longer I was in a relationship, the more of myself—my energy, my time, my affection, and my emotion—I poured into the guy I was dating. We would stay on the phone for hours each night, discussing dreams, fears, and desires, and declaring our love and passion for each other. We would spend every minute of our free time together. Between classes we could be found in the hallway entangled in each other's arms. Lots of times, I felt like I was all but married to the guy I was dating. I told him everything, and I gave him nearly everything. I built my world around him in every possible way.

Our Inner Treasure

It comes naturally for women to pour ourselves into a relationship, to become emotionally wrapped up in the guy we like, to revolve our world around him. That's not always true with a guy. A man may not be as tempted to open his heart to someone; in fact, he may not even know how. He doesn't usually build his life around the girl he's dating. It's very common for a guy to get involved physically without getting involved emotionally at all.

A familiar scenario during high school was the girl who came to me in tears, devastated because she had given herself away emotionally and physically to a guy, only to find out later that he was just using her for sex. She thought he loved her. He thought she was easy prey.

And then came another scenario as I grew older, this one a little more surprising. Instead of girls letting themselves be used like sex objects by guys, the girls became the ones who went out looking for a conquest.

"He's so hot. I think I'll have sex with him this weekend," was a casual comment I often heard, usually communicated in terms just a little more graphic.

They shut off their emotions. They subconsciously told themselves that the only way to be protected from heartbreak was to deny they had a heart and revert to the same animalistic, noncommittal attitude toward sex they had seen in guys.

This emotionless mind-set toward sex has caused an enormous mess in modern relationships. Dating relationships are being replaced with meaningless one-hour sexual trysts with total strangers. Girls who get emotional about sex—expecting guys to call them afterward or wanting a serious relationship first—are scoffed at as immature and weak. All too many young women have adopted the attitude that if they ignore their feminine heart and desires and become "guy-like" in their sexuality, they will be more in control and less vulnerable to heartache.

But any girl who has tried this approach will admit, if she's honest, that it just doesn't work. In fact, shutting off our feminine emotions only creates *more* pain and confusion. As women, we are *designed* to give ourselves completely—emotionally and physically—to *one* man. And we have a deep need to be loved and cherished for a lifetime by the man to whom we give that gift.

Physical purity can't be separated from our emotions. It's a package deal. When we give ourselves to someone emotionally, it leads right to the next step: giving ourselves to him physically.

I will never forget hearing an unmarried friend of mine describe why she gave her virginity away to a guy she'd been in love with for years. "I gave my heart to Matt," she told me. "I poured my life into him. I couldn't imagine giving my virginity to anyone else—he already had the rest of me, so I decided to give him the whole package."

Even if we try to set our emotions aside and merely "conquer" a guy physically, whether we like it or not, our emotions *do* get involved. Trying to ignore that delicate, vulnerable, and emotional part of us is to deny the very fabric of our being as women.

Maybe you have learned the hard lesson that casually giving yourself away physically causes incredible pain—you feel guilty, dirty, and used afterwards. But have you ever thought of your *heart* as a treasure every bit as valuable as your physical purity?

Priceless Pearl

As women, we are given a great gift: our purity. It is like a priceless pearl, tucked safely away in a protective shell, growing and becoming more beautiful with time. Our purity is so much more than just our physical virginity; it starts with who we are on the *inside*. Everything that makes us who we are emotionally—our feminine nature, our sensitivity, our vulnerability, and our desire to give ourselves fully to one man—is part of that gift.

Have you ever felt the pain that comes from casually giving away your heart? From pouring all of yourself into someone, only to have that precious treasure thrown onto the ground and trampled?

In my dating relationships, I damaged my precious pearl of purity. But the damage didn't just happen when I gave too much of myself physically. Giving away this treasure started the moment I gave away my heart and emotions to men who were never meant to receive that gift. I had been careless with my treasure. I had *allowed* my heart to become battered and broken.

I used to think the unbearable devastation of breaking up with a boyfriend was just a natural part of the dating process. But there was nothing natural about it. It was a pain God never meant for me to experience. The valuable and delicate pearl of my purity had been ripped too soon from its protective shell, then tossed aside, damaged and bruised.

As Carrie, a distraught sophomore in college, described it, "I've been in so many relationships and been hurt so many times that my heart is nothing but hamburger meat now."

I can relate to that statement. In fact, I don't know many girls who haven't been through a "hamburger heart" experience.

All the Days of My Life

Not long after my decision to "give God the pen" to write my love story, I learned a truth about loving my future husband that dramatically changed the way I was living as a single young woman.

I was innocently reading my "proverb for the day," which happened to be Proverbs 31, the famous chapter in the Bible that describes the "wife of godly character."

I must admit I wasn't paying very close attention or taking the words too seriously. After all, I figured most of it wouldn't apply to me until *after* I was a wife, which as far as I was concerned, wouldn't be for a while. Then suddenly these words stood out to me:

She [the wife of godly character] does him [her husband] good
and not evil all the days of her life. (Proverbs 31:12)

Wait a minute, I thought. *All the days of her life?* What was that supposed to mean? I had yet to meet any woman who had been married *all* the days of her life. Did this verse mean she tried to do her husband good…even *before* she met him?

I felt a gentle nudge on my heart. And somehow, I knew this was

what God wanted for me: to seek my future husband's highest good—
starting right now.

How can I love someone I've never met? I argued inwardly. *I'm saving my virginity for my future husband. I don't even know the guy. So
what else can I possibly do for him?*

The gentle nudge continued, ultimately forcing me to examine the
way I was living. How had I been approaching relationships? Each time
I was involved with someone, I poured my heart, my emotions, my
affection, my time, and all my attention into that person. Not to mention the fact that, although I technically remained a virgin, I wasn't keeping myself physically pure. I was constantly compromising my standards.

How would my future husband feel, I wondered, *if he could see me
pouring myself into these relationships? If he could watch me freely giving
away my heart, my emotions, and even most of my physical purity to guy
after guy?*

I had to face a shocking realization: I really had *not* been keeping
myself pure at all. I had been taking the treasure of my heart and emotions and spending it carelessly on temporary relationships. My heart
ached as I thought about it. I realized so clearly that I hadn't been loving my future husband with the way I had been living. I hadn't even
been considering him at all. Instead, I had been consumed with meeting my own immediate desires. Sadness overcame me as I saw that I
had been giving a treasure that belonged to him, piece by piece, to
each guy I dated.

How much of your treasure will be left, came a soft whisper to my
heart, *if you continue to give it away, piece by piece, in one relationship
after another?*

I knew that eventually I would meet my future husband and that I would want to love him with all that was in me. But how could I offer my whole heart to my husband someday if it was nothing but a used, battered, and broken mess?

"Lord, I want to truly love my future husband with the way I live," I decided, "and I am making a commitment today to love him and seek his highest good from now on, to live as if he can see my every thought and action and to honor him in every way possible."

True Love

Once I committed to stop chasing after emotional and physical passion, my eyes were opened to another love, a higher love that *is* strong enough to build a lifelong relationship upon. It is, in fact, the very same love God demonstrated for us when He sacrificed His only Son

I have chosen to not pursue any serious relationship with a guy until God decides that it is time. I'm not ignorant—I know what the rest of my generation is doing. My friends are all getting married or at least in serious relationships. But I know that until I am satisfied with only God, I cannot truly love a guy as He designed me to. God is working in me, teaching me to love Him as my one true Prince and to see the Christian guys around me as fellow pilgrims, not "potentials." I am constantly reminding myself that my future husband is alive right now and thinking about what I'll tell him someday about how I lived my life before I met him.

COURTNEY J., AGE 23

to die in our place. And it is not based on feelings or physical desires. It is based on a *choice,* a commitment that says, "I will seek your highest good above my own. I will lay down my life for you."

When Eric and I promised each other we would stay together for life—no matter if he loses his hair and gets a belly, or if I burn all his meals—we knew we could keep this commitment because it was based not on feelings but on a *choice.*

Don't get me wrong. Passion, emotion, and physical attraction are fun and exciting aspects of any healthy relationship. But in our culture, passionate emotions and physical desires are the sole basis for almost every romantic relationship. No wonder marriages are crumbling left and right!

We need to think of passion as merely the icing on the cake—it's what adds that extra dimension of flavor to a relationship. But it's not the ingredient that keeps a romance together. If we don't have a lasting love for and commitment to our spouse as the foundation of our relationship, we don't have anything at all.

If anyone should know how to give lasting love, it should be Christians. We have the very example of Jesus Christ Himself on which to pattern our lives and our love toward others. We have the Great Lover Himself enabling us to love like He does! Why do we so often neglect pouring that kind of love into our love life?

Love That Lasts Through the Storms

Soon after Eric and I became engaged, some mutual friends introduced us to one of the most extraordinary examples of commitment-love we've ever seen. Karen and Scott had been happily married for about ten years when something happened that changed their lives forever. Scott, a respected businessman, was driving to work when he collided with a large truck pulling a two-ton trailer. In the accident, the trailer landed on top of his car, pinning him underneath. He suffered a severe blow to the head.

At the hospital, Karen learned that Scott had extensive brain damage. He would no longer be able to think or communicate as an adult. In fact, he didn't even remember who she was at first.

Over the following weeks and months, Karen had to adjust to seeing her husband confined to a wheelchair and speaking and acting like a child. He had to be fed, washed, and dressed. He was no longer the capable man she had married.

Most of us wouldn't have blamed Karen if she had chosen to put Scott into a nursing home and gotten on with her life. After all, he could no longer meet any of her needs, and it placed a huge burden on her to care for him in this condition.

But as Karen puts it, "I remembered that on our wedding day I had made a commitment to Scott…and a commitment isn't meant to be broken."

So for years, she has faithfully served Scott, loving him even when he didn't remember her, helping him when he couldn't help her back. Today, Scott has made tremendous progress in his condition, yet he remains physically impaired. He is always in need of Karen's love, help, and support, and she faithfully gives it. How incredibly beautiful! This is heroic Christlike love in action. This is the kind of love Christian marriages should be made of. Their example gave Eric and me such a powerful real-life picture of unconditional love and reminded us what the foundation of our relationship must always be.

A Simple Glass of Water

Unconditional love can be demonstrated in far less dramatic ways as well. Since Eric and I have been married, I have offered him plenty of opportunities to test his unconditional love for me. He has seen my most selfish moments. He has seen me when I look my very worst… and he still loves me!

When I was pregnant with our son, Hudson, it seemed that almost every night, just as Eric drifted off to sleep, I would get hungry or thirsty. Since it had taken me fifteen minutes to find a comfortable position, I dreaded the idea of having to get out of bed to go get some crackers from downstairs. So in my very best pitiful puppy-dog voice I would say, "Sweets? I need some food and a glass of water."

Eric could have easily pretended to be asleep or simply mumbled, "Well, why don't you just go get some then?" But every time, he chose a higher path. After a groggy "Huh? Um…okay," he heroically arose from the warm bed and staggered to the kitchen to get me a snack. No complaints. No grumbling. Just pure, unconditional love in action.

I wouldn't recommend putting unconditional love to the test just for the fun of it. I try not to take advantage of Eric's amazing servant's heart. But it is wonderful to know that our relationship is based on that kind of love…for a lifetime.

Most people, even Christians, take their own selfish agendas into marriage, and reap the dismal results. But when two people are fully surrendered to Jesus Christ and consumed with loving and honoring Him with every breath they take, it sets the stage for a romance that rivals the fairy tales.

A God-scripted marriage *is* more than worth waiting for. If you live to honor your spouse with every thought, word, action, and friendship *all the days of your life,* you will unlock the secret to the kind of love you've always longed for.

> Keep your heart with all diligence, for out of it spring the issues of life.
>
> PROVERBS 4:23

> The King's daughter is all glorious within; her clothing is interwoven with gold.
>
> PSALM 45:13 (NASB)

A Look Inside Your Heart

1. What evidence have you personally seen that emotional flings do not adequately prepare a person for marriage? Why do you think so many people pursue short-lived romantic relationships?

2. How would you describe the difference between passion and love?

3. In what ways have you put your heart at risk? In the future, how can you guard your physical *and* emotional purity?

4. What are some practical ways you can begin loving your future spouse all the days of your life, starting right now?

A Step Further

Have you ever seriously examined the way you relate to the opposite sex? Why not set aside some time today to consider what you've read in this chapter. Are you in the habit of giving your heart, mind, and emotions away to one person after the next? If so, what changes do you need to make? Are you willing to set your entire life aside—body, mind, and heart—for the person you will one day marry? Prayerfully consider this decision, then write out your commitment to your future spouse. Keep it in a special place where you can be reminded of your decision. If God's plan for you is marriage, one day it will be a valuable treasure you can offer to the one you will spend the rest of your life with.

Seven

Beyond Technical Virginity

A female angle on protecting what's sacred

✗ LESLIE ✗

I was thirteen the first time a guy asked me to have sex with him. I had known Bryan, a cocky soccer-playing fifteen-year-old, for approximately two days when he called me up out of the blue with a "romantic proposition." It went something like this.

"Hi, Lisa," he mumbled while smacking loudly on a potato chip.

"My name's *Leslie*," I corrected.

"Oh yeah. Sorry, I forgot," he floundered as he stifled a burp. "Anyway, I really like you and I was just wondering, when do you think we can have sex?"

It was not exactly the fairy-tale scenario I'd always dreamed of. Bryan was about as far as was humanly possible from being the heroic Prince Charming of my girlhood longings. And yet part of me was secretly happy that a guy was attracted enough to actually want to have sex with me.

Elementary school had taken its toll on my self-esteem. Lots of girls seemed able to sail blissfully through childhood without attracting any negative male attention. Unfortunately, I was not one of them. Boys started telling me I was ugly and undesirable from about fourth grade on. The pressure I felt to make myself sexually attractive—even at the age of ten—was incredibly intense. Since then I'd worked hard to follow the examples of pop culture, wearing tighter clothes and adopting a sensual flirtatious attitude around the opposite sex. Finally, my efforts had begun paying off.

Bryan's proposition certainly wasn't the ideal kind of male attention. Still, it was far better than being mocked, ridiculed, and discarded as sexually inferior by all the guys my age.

I wasn't really tempted to give away my virginity to a lowlife like Bryan. As I said earlier, I'd been raised on a healthy dose of the abstinence philosophy. Growing up in church, I'd been taught that "true love waits." But the older I got, the more I began to question whether the "just don't have sex before marriage" message I got at church was based in reality.

In the world I lived in, sexual temptation wasn't something that just lurked around dark corners; sexual temptation was constantly in your face. The school hallways were littered with couples passionately kissing and groping each other against their lockers; guys telling graphic porn jokes and bellowing with obnoxious laughter; guys and girls flirting, teasing, and grabbing each other; and school nurses dutifully handing out condoms to anyone who seemed to be on the brink of engaging in casual sex, which included the vast majority of my classmates. In my world, the only reason someone would graduate from high school a virgin was if he or she was a complete social outcast.

Nearly all of my friends told me about their sexual exploits on a regular basis. I knew couples at school who would go to their cars during lunch or breaks and have sex during the school day. And of course, every party I went to was all about going off with your latest fling to experiment sexually. In the classrooms, on the bus, in the halls, and everywhere else, girls would be touched and grabbed by guys in ways that would have utterly shocked our parents. Yet most of us encouraged this kind of warped male attention. From what I could see, becoming a sex object was far better than being mocked and rejected by guys. Any girl trying to keep her purity was disregarded and labeled a prude…and was totally undesirable to every guy she encountered.

The Abstinence Approach

In the midst of all this, there came a wave of Christian teaching about purity in the form of abstinence seminars, books with guidelines for "Christian dating," and promise rings. It came in many different packages, but the basic message went something like this: "Kids, don't have sex before marriage. You need to respect yourself and your future spouse. Sex will be so much more beautiful if you wait till marriage. Protect yourself from STDs, pregnancy, and heartache. Abstinence is cool! Thousands of young people are committed to waiting. Why don't you wait too?"

Somewhere along the way, between my mom and dad's parental exhortation and my youth pastor's "purity pep rallies," I got the message that my virginity was a treasure to save for my future husband. I tried to believe that someday there would be a man who would appreciate the fact that I had remained a virgin for him. Even though I didn't see one eligible guy in my life who seemed to want a pure young woman, I was assured men like that did exist.

As I described in previous chapters, early in my dating life I made a commitment to purity, heroically declaring, "I'm not gonna have sex till marriage." I hoped my husband would appreciate such a sacrifice someday! In the meantime, I was going to go out there and date for fun, live it up, have a great time, go to the edge, enjoy relationships, and then later down the road I'd meet Mr. Right and forget about every other boyfriend I'd ever had. I was sure that as long as I didn't have sex, surely my future husband, parents, church leaders, and even God would have to be impressed.

All this time I thought of myself as pure because I was holding on (barely) to my virginity. Whenever I was with a guy, I tried to make sure the guy I went out with shared the same conviction.

"Yeah, of course I believe in abstinence until marriage too," they always assured me with an irresistible smile before we launched into a passionate make-out session.

But I didn't feel pure. Deep down, nothing about these temporary, shallow dating relationships felt right. I had always longed for a knight in shining armor to sweep me off my feet, to cherish me like a princess, to honor me. As a starry-eyed young girl, I had expected dating to be a beautiful, romantic experience in which I would feel treasured and loved.

This animalistic, physical passion from guys who did not truly know me or care about me was *not* the fulfillment of my romantic dreams. I didn't feel cherished. I felt used. I felt dirty. Especially those times when I had given so much of myself to a relationship, and then after it ended, I had to see that guy with another girl, ignoring me as if I didn't exist.

In spite of how those in my Christian circles equated purity with virginity, I began to realize there *had* to be more to it than just not having sex. Otherwise, I wouldn't feel so defiled every time I gave my heart and physical body to a guy. I had thought of "losing my purity" as a forbidden line I was never to cross—the edge of the cliff. But after painful reflection, the truth burned deep into my heart: in getting as close to the edge as I possibly could, I had lost something precious already.

My entire perspective on purity changed the day I committed to truly loving my future husband with the way I lived. I realized that real purity was far more than just trying not to fall off the edge of a cliff. It wasn't just trying to *technically* stay a virgin until marriage. Rather, purity was a lifestyle. It meant living to love and honor my future husband *all the days of my life*—with my thoughts, my actions, my words, my emotions, and my body.

That decision transformed my love life and my interactions with guys. Even though I didn't know him yet, I began truly loving Eric at that moment. From that point on, I no longer built my life around the pursuit of the opposite sex. My focus was on building my relationship with Christ and waiting faithfully for the man He would bring into my life one day. I didn't jump into temporary flings anymore. I stopped flirting and seeking to draw guys' attention. I stopped dressing seductively to draw guys' approving glances. I became more guarded in my friendships with guys, no longer carelessly showcasing my deepest thoughts and desires to those who were not meant to see my innermost heart. I no longer spent my free time cavorting and socializing with guys.

Yes, I did have guy friends. But they were not the casual flirting, teasing, tickling, and joking kind of friendships I'd always had before. Rather, I built friendships with guys who were far more focused on Jesus Christ than on pursuing girls. They were waiting faithfully for their future wives and did not see me as a potential girlfriend. We were able to have pure, unpretentious brother-sister friendships, continually pointing each other toward Christ instead of drawing attention to ourselves. Rather than constantly trying to get me to lower my standards, they were protective of my inward and outward purity. They never tempted me to offer my heart, body, or emotions to them; in fact, they probably would not have been comfortable having a friendship with me if I had carelessly given them what was meant only for my future husband. I was delighted to learn that it was possible to have this kind of pure friendship with a member of the opposite sex. Before these friendships, I hadn't realized Christ-focused guys like this even existed. It wasn't until I began honoring and loving my future husband with every aspect of my life that I began to meet guys who were living the same way for their future wives. As I described in my book *Authentic Beauty*:

> Looking back, it makes sense. Why would someone with
> higher standards take any notice of me, when I had been
> spending all my energy proving to the world that I was just
> like every other careless young woman out there, throwing my
> heart, mind, and body to guy after guy? But when I began to
> carefully guard my femininity and live differently than the
> other young women of the culture, guys who were committed
> to living differently started to come out of the woodwork.[1]

It was wonderful to have healthy, Christ-centered, pure friendships with godly guys. But even so, I remained guarded about what I shared with them, how much time I spent with them, and what kind of physical touch I engaged in with them. In fact, there was really no physical touch in the friendships at all—even casual hugs—because I didn't want to open the door for any kind of distraction or temptation. I felt strongly that every part of my mind, heart, and body from now on was to be kept sacred for the one man I would spend the rest of my life with.

Worth Waiting For

I know this kind of commitment might seem unrealistic. Our entire society is based upon the pursuit of the opposite sex. We are programmed to derive our confidence from the approval of the opposite sex. The Christian world is no different. I can't count the number of times Eric and I have attended a church gathering of teens, college students, or young singles and seen an environment based on flirting, cavorting, tickling, and teasing. Guys tickling girls. Girls playfully tackling guys. Guys bellowing loud greetings and giving girls bear hugs. Girls giggling and jumping on guys' backs. This kind of guy/girl interaction is completely accepted in our Christian culture. In a world where it's normal to have sex with a complete stranger, a little playful flirting and cavorting hardly seems like a big deal.

But what does God think?

It is good for a man not to touch a woman. (1 Corinthians 7:1)

Although some translations interpret this verse as "it is good for a man not to marry," in reality the word *touch* here means "physical contact." It's the same word used all throughout the New Testament for every kind of touch, even casual. Physical touch between men and women is very powerful, not something to be treated flippantly. Our Christian culture may make light of casual touch between guys and girls, but it's not a light thing to God. Our Maker designed physical touch between men and women to be the catalyst for sexual intimacy, and when that fire is ignited out of context, it leads to harm. As it says in Proverbs:

> Can a man take fire to his bosom, and his clothes not be
> burned? Can one walk on hot coals, and his feet not be seared?
> (Proverbs 6:27–28)

God designed emotional, physical, and sensual interaction to be kept sacred for marriage. His intent was not to make us miserable but to help us experience the fullness, beauty, and mystery of married love as He created it to be. The entire book of Song of Solomon paints a vivid picture of the delights and beauty of married love. According to God's design, *every* expression of love, emotion, and physical desire should be treated as sacred, savored and treasured by one man and one woman within a lifelong marriage covenant.

I realize that modern marriage doesn't seem worth waiting for. Why forgo the pleasure of passion while we are young and single, only to end up with a mediocre, passionless marriage in which the romance dies after the honeymoon? With the divorce rate among Christians just as high as the rest of society, we certainly aren't seeing many examples of lifelong love. But when a love story is put together by God Himself—when He remains at the center of a romance—it only grows more beautiful with time.

"I'm Already Taken"

As I said earlier, purity involves more than just avoiding the forbidden line of giving away our virginity. It's keeping our heart, mind, and body sacred and set apart for the one person we will spend the rest of our lives with.

It may seem impossible to live that way in this day of high school orgies and no-strings hookups. But as we discussed in chapter 5, purity is not something we are required to live out on our own strength. If Jesus Christ is the central focus of our lives, He provides power to be victorious in areas where we would fail on our own.

Annie, one of my close friends, is a beautiful brunette with a radiant smile. Her concept of purity growing up was completely different from mine. At twenty-five, she has never been in a dating relationship, never given her heart away, never even been kissed. It might sound extreme, but Annie is far from miserable. Instead, she's one of the most fulfilled young women I know.

Annie decided from a young age that she wanted to offer a treasure of purity to her husband on her wedding day. But this was not just another "abstinence commitment." This was a choice to carefully guard her heart, her emotions, her physical purity, and everything she was, for the man she would one day marry. Her goal is to offer herself fully and completely, with no excess baggage, to her husband someday.

During her youth, she allowed her Maker to care for and develop that precious pearl of her purity so it would become a sparkling, glistening, and untarnished gem for her husband. And she asked her Lord to guard and protect her delicate heart in His hands.

She is not a social misfit. She is confident in who she is, enthusiastic about life, and comfortable around guys. Because Annie has been so careful with her treasure, she's not tempted to blow such a valuable gift on just any guy who shows interest in her. The man she marries is going to have to *win* her heart first.

"As for guys pursuing me for temporary relationships," she says, "my attitude is 'I'm already taken.' Until God brings my future husband along and I know he's the one, I'm not available."

What a difference from the attitude I had when I was haphazardly throwing my heart around like a Nerf ball. My precious pearl had been up for grabs to anyone who caught my eye, and as a result, it did not reach its full potential for beauty. Annie, on the other hand, has tucked her treasure safely into the hands of God, not to be retrieved until He shows her it's time.

It's not that Annie has never made a mistake. It's not that she has never struggled with living out her commitment. She will be the first to admit that she is very human. She deals with the same frustrations, temptations, fears, and doubts we all have. There are moments of extreme loneliness. She has wondered at times if her standards are too high, if her commitment is really worth it. And she acknowledges that the only thing that has gotten her this far has been leaning heavily upon her Savior each and every day.

But her decision represents the kind of standard we all should strive for, with God's help. *Becoming a one-man woman.* Loving our future husbands with the way we live and the way we guard our pearl of purity…*all the days of our lives.* Not out of obligation, but out of unconditional love for our future spouse and a deep desire to honor our Maker.

Two people who have saved themselves completely—inwardly, outwardly, emotionally, and physically—coming together to love each other for a lifetime with the purest, most uninhibited love imaginable…this is romance in its truest form. This is God's perfect design for you. This is the "sweeter song." And it's something you can begin to work toward right now!

Many of us have damaged our pearl of purity or even given away

Something that really helps me remain faithful to my future spouse is limiting the movies I watch. This has been hard, because I don't get much support from other people when I say why I don't watch certain things. But I realize that chick flicks filled with cute guys and "perfect" love stories can easily cause me to focus on a guy's outward appearance rather than his heart for God. Those kinds of movies influenced me toward the world's way of thinking about romance, rather than God's, and gave me false definitions of what a true man and true woman should look like. The Lord has been teaching me that romance is His idea—not Hollywood's—and that the world's version of love is like a single drop of rain compared to the ocean of blessing He wants to give me, if I will entrust this area of my life completely to Him.

ERIKA, AGE 24

our treasure completely. If this is your story, it's not too late, by the grace of God, to start walking a different path. It's not too late to discover a God-written love story. It's time to allow God to mold you into His likeness.

Through God's miraculous, redeeming work in my life, I had a full, undamaged gift of purity to offer to Eric on my wedding day. God is in the business of making all things new. All we must do is turn and, by His grace, walk a different direction.

What a Real Man Wants

"But what if there isn't a guy out there who really *wants* a woman of purity?"

This question haunts nearly every Christian young woman I've encountered.

And I understand why. In our culture, purity in any way, shape, or form is not valued, at least not by most men. We are persuaded to think that men like easy women and they don't want to waste their time with those who play hard to get.

It seems that for every woman I know who has made a commitment to purity, one of her biggest struggles is that men are always trying to get her to lower her standards. Even most Christian men do not seem to fully appreciate a woman's desire to guard her heart and protect her purity. It's an unending battle for a woman to hold on to her treasure, and then she begins to wonder if it's even worth it. What if guys really *aren't* looking for that kind of purity in a woman?

Before Eric and I were married, God brought a handful of Christ-focused young men into my life as friends. It was amazing to see the way in which they honored their future wives. I remember one particular conversation I had with them in which they described what they were looking for in a woman. It went something like this:

"A woman who has mystery—who guards her heart and isn't easy to get."

"A woman with backbone. High standards. Different from this culture."

"A woman who is focused on God and isn't easily distracted by men."

"A woman who doesn't throw herself at me, but allows me to win her heart over time."

I couldn't resist asking a few questions.

"So do you guys all want a woman who is committed to purity?"

A chorus of emphatic affirmative responses filled the air.

"And what's your opinion of girls who are easy?"

"It's disgusting."

"A turnoff."

"Totally unattractive."

"How do you feel about a girl who is careful about guarding her emotions?"

"I have the utmost respect for a girl like that."

"That's the kind of girl I'd want to marry."

"If I'm interested in a girl, it may be frustrating if she doesn't fall for me right away, but deep down I am all the more intrigued by the challenge of winning her heart."

These are *real* responses from *real* men. What I have discovered as Eric and I have traveled this country is that the kind of men who are worth waiting for really *do* exist. And they really *are* looking for a woman who values purity. I have since had similar discussions with hundreds of eligible Christ-focused young men of real integrity. And I have yet to meet one who is *not* longing for a woman of true purity. Men who go after easy women for another "score" are just looking to feed their flesh. They are not looking for true love, and they certainly aren't worthy of your time and attention.

A *real* man, the kind of man a woman wants to give her life to, is one who will respect her dignity, who will honor her like the valuable treasure she is. A *real* man will not attempt to rip her precious pearl from its protective shell or persuade her with charm to give away her treasure prematurely. He will wait patiently until she willingly gives him the prize of her heart. A *real* man will cherish and care for that precious prize forever.

It's unfortunate that women have to work overtime just to protect their hearts these days. If we had more *real* men who treat women as God intended, it wouldn't be so difficult! But even if real men are hard to find, they do exist, and they are worth waiting for. So don't get discouraged on your journey toward inward excellence. To real men, your purity is *beautiful,* and it will be highly esteemed someday.

I once heard a Christlike guy capture well what a *real* man is looking for in a woman when he declared, "I don't want a woman who just turns my head, but a woman who turns my *heart*."

Just think, if God has planned marriage for your life, there is one real man who might be dreaming of a woman who is waiting faithfully for him at this very moment.

Promise me, O women of Jerusalem, by the gazelles and wild
deer, not to awaken love until the time is right.

SONG OF SONGS 2:7 (NLT)

Flee also youthful lusts; but pursue righteousness, faith, love,
peace with those who call on the Lord out of a pure heart.

2 TIMOTHY 2:22

[Treat] younger women as sisters, with all purity.

1 TIMOTHY 5:2

A Look Inside Your Heart

1. What is the difference between technical virginity and true
   purity?
2. Which, if any, of your current relationships with the opposite sex are based on a shared value of purity in heart, mind,
   and body? What friendships and relationships might you
   need to give up in order to honor your future spouse? Are
   you willing to do so?
3. When you think forward to marriage, what are some
   of the ways you envision that relationship being different
   from any other? How might the choices you make as a
   single person affect your later enjoyment of married
   delights?
4. What choices can you make, starting today, to be a one-
   woman man or a one-man woman?

A Step Further

Have you allowed Christ to shape you into a woman of purity, or is your femininity being shaped by the culture's influence? If you have not guarded your pearl of purity for your husband up until now, hope is not lost. You can make a choice today, by God's grace, to turn and walk a different way. Write down a detailed description of the kind of young woman you desire to be—both for Christ and for your future husband. Then ask God to equip you with the strength to live it out.

Part Three

The Training Ground

*Practical Preparation for a God-Written
Love Story*

Eight

Romantic Heroism

A skill to learn long before the wedding vows

✖ ERIC ✖

I remember learning the basics of how not to treat a girl when I was seven. Her name was Emily—a neighbor girl from down the street—and she was "yuck!" Nasty little Emily was solely responsible for scribbling on my 1978 Denver Broncos team picture. She was also the intolerable human being who called me a doofhead in front of my good buddy Stevie.

I'll never forget the lecture I received from my mom, only moments after I belted wicked little Emily with my plastic light saber.

"Eric!" my mom scolded while squeezing my scrawny little arm, "you should *never,* and I mean NEVER, hit a girl!"

"But she called me a doofhead!" I protested with a face as red as Superman's cape.

"I don't care what she called you! A young man should NEVER hit a girl!" With that very clear message reverberating through my cranium, I spent the rest of the day in my room staring forlornly at my graffiti-scrawled Broncos picture. But all was not lost. I learned a valuable lesson in chivalry that miserable day.

As the years passed, I added to my repertoire of valuable lessons in chivalry. Little blond Rebecca's bloodcurdling screams helped teach me *never* to pull the legs off a crawdad in a lady's presence. Then there was Priscilla, the little varmint with red curls from down the street, who helped me understand the virtue of using Lysol to cover guyish fragrances in the "potty room."

By the age of eleven I had learned enough valuable lessons to prevent a girl from fleeing for her life when coming within a hundred feet of me. But I still had a lot to learn when it came to truly romancing a woman.

Future lessons were even more painful, but by the age of twenty, I was starting to catch on to this "gentleman" thing. It was Leslie who actually taught me most of what I know when it comes to true chivalry and romantic goodness.

Rule no. 1: *Always* and *instantaneously* notice when a woman gets her hair cut.

Rule no. 2: Be a keen observer of how her earrings draw out the sparkle in her lovely eyes. And finally…

Rule no. 3: Periodically stop at rest-room facilities, without being asked, if ever on a trip longer than sixty-two minutes with a woman in the car.

If young men would just put into practice those three things, I think the divorce rate in the next generation of marriages would drop 5 percent. But as a revolutionary romantic, a measly 5 percent doesn't get me excited. I would love to see men begin to sweetly cherish women, and women tenderly honor men the way God designed them to. But unfortunately, just adding a few chivalrous characteristics to our love lives won't accomplish *that,* and it certainly won't bring the melody of the "sweeter song" into our romantic relationships.

If we really are after the beautiful side of love, the version of romance that would make Hollywood's collective chin drop to the floor, then we need to pursue becoming a lover like the Great Lover Himself. We need to seek to reflect the goodness of our great God. He was not only a Lover who laid down His life for His Bride and kept Himself spotlessly pure in heart, mind, and body; He was also a Lover who was wholly faithful. In other words, Jesus knew how to blend His love and purity with patience. He knew how to be single with purpose, in a way that would honor and cherish His future Bride.

If we learn to mirror Jesus's faithfulness in how we relate to our future spouse, I guarantee the word *divorce* will become a dusty old term that up-and-coming generations won't even know how to define.

It's an Art

Faithfulness is an extremely misunderstood attribute of heavenly romance. How can you be faithful to someone *before* you even meet? Isn't faithfulness a quality that becomes important once a relationship already exists?

Well, just as Norman Rockwell could have never expected to paint a timeless masterpiece if he'd never taken an art lesson in his entire life, neither can you expect to master the art of faithfulness if you wait until the wedding bells chime to start practicing it.

Though only a few can be successful at painting a timeless master-piece on a canvas, we are *all* commanded by God to be successful in mastering the art of faithfulness. Faithfulness is a discipline that is refined and honed through years of practice. In a sense, faithfulness means developing the habit of loving your future spouse through patiently waiting, consistently hoping, and living by the high standard to which you've been called. I like to picture faithfulness as an oak tree that patiently endures the torrid winds and rains, only to become stronger and more solid as a result. It is strength learned through persevering; it is integrity gained through waiting. It's imperative to the beautiful side of love.

> *I believe that God will bring my future wife to me in His perfect timing. I pray for my spouse and ask God to make her far more consumed with following after Christ than chasing after me. That prayer helps me stay on track in my own life—running after Christ rather than the things the world offers, and knowing He will take care of the rest.*
>
> PADDEN, AGE 21

Habits

When we are in diapers, we begin to establish habitual patterns. Break-fast at four in the morning, doo-doo at five, temper tantrum at six, bottle at seven, doo-doo at eight, hit doggy at nine, doo-doo at ten, scribble on wall at eleven, and finally, to cap off the eventful morning, throw squash in Mommy's hair at noon.

As all mommies know, if you are not trained to develop new habits as a toddler, you will not only become an obnoxious adult, but you will still be throwing temper tantrums at the age of twenty-six.

When most of us think of habits, we think of brushing our teeth, locking the front door before going to bed, praying before meals, or— my favorite—staring absent-mindedly into the refrigerator when I can't remember what it was Leslie asked me to do.

Well, let's expand our horizons a little and invite faithfulness into our definition of habits. Because, not only is faithfulness a bona fide habit, it's the chief habit—both in our love life with our future spouse and in our love life with Jesus, our Great Lover and our King.

Just imagine that inside your heart is a place where only one person can ever enter, other than God. This place is a combination between a minikingdom where you store up your finest treasures and a dazzling meadow where your sweetest flowers bloom. In this minikingdom you store up the most extravagant love, and in this dazzling meadow you nurture your most tender affections. The longer this sanctuary is faithfully guarded, cultivated, and beautified, the more enchanting it will become.

Another Greek Tale

Once upon a time there lived a beautiful queen named Penelope who was carefully weaving a white linen roll. (Don't ask me what a white linen roll actually *is*; I assume it's some kind of decorative doily.) It was to be a gift for her husband whose return she anxiously awaited each day. (Why he'd want a doily, I don't know. This is one of the great mysteries of Greek mythology as far as I'm concerned.) For years the king had been away fighting in the Trojan War. Each and every day Penelope would say his name over and over again, somehow hoping he would hear the cry of her aching heart.

One day, many great chiefs and princes, all in search of wives, set sail for Ithaca to try to win Penelope's hand. They assured the lonely queen that the king had died in battle, and that it would be best for the people of Ithaca and for her own protection that she pick one of them to be her new husband.

But Penelope, with tears in her royal eyes, answered, "Heroes and most honored princes, I refuse to believe what you say. I am certain that my noble husband lives, and I must faithfully keep his kingdom for him till he returns. I am weaving a white linen roll for him even now."

The chiefs and princes stubbornly refused to return home and daily reminded her of her need for a husband and of Ithaca's need for a king.

Weeks passed by, and still Penelope did not bend but continued to faithfully weave her linen roll in hopes of the king's return. The chiefs and princes tried every possible persuasion, but to no avail. The group of hopeful suitors moved into the palace, drinking the royal wine and consuming the royal food. They refused to depart until Penelope chose one of them to marry.

A weary and reluctant Penelope finally agreed to choose a new husband as soon as she finished weaving her white linen roll, if the king had not returned by then. Weeks passed, and still she kept weaving. However, by night she would secretly unravel all the thread she had woven during the day. Eventually her scheme was discovered.

A leader among them, Agelaus, called the assembly together and addressed Penelope in a loud voice. "Queen Penelope," he fumed angrily, "your stubbornness has left us no choice but to take this matter into our own hands. We have seen your trickery in delaying the completion of your cursed linen roll, and we will stand for it no longer. Finish it by tomorrow and select your new husband before noon, or we will choose him for you! We will not wait another day!"

The next afternoon all the suitors gathered to await Penelope's decision. Just as she entered the banquet hall, a strange beggar quietly crept into the assembly. His head was hidden beneath a tattered hood, and a ragged cloak was wrapped around his decrepit body. He hobbled to the back of the hall quietly, unnoticed save for a few mocking sneers from the suitors he passed. Penelope began to speak, capturing the attention of all present.

"Chiefs and Princes," said Penelope with a knot of grief in her regal throat, "we will leave this decision to fate. Behold, I am holding the great bow of my husband, the king. Each of you must try your strength in bending it, and I will choose the one amongst you who can shoot the most accurate arrow."

"Agreed!" cried the suitors, and they eagerly lined up to test their strength.

One after the other struggled to bend the great bow. Then losing patience, each of the gallant nobles threw it to the ground and strode away.

"Only a giant could bend that bow of iron!" they moaned.

"Perhaps the filthy old beggar would like to test his strength," one yelled with a sneer.

At that, the beggar rose from his chair and moved with halting steps to the head of the hall.

"You old fool!" the suitors howled in derision as the dirty traveler picked up the great bow.

Suddenly a remarkable change came over the stranger. The decrepit traveler straightened his back and rose to his full height, and even in a beggar's rags it was impossible not to notice that this weary traveler was every inch a *king*. Then, without effort, he bent the bow and strung it as everyone in the great hall looked on in astonishment. The king had returned!

The suitors were speechless. Then, in sheer panic, they turned and

I keep a journal for my future wife. I jot down loves letters, poems, etc. I write as if she's a real person, not some ambiguous entity in some foggy alternate universe! I know that she's alive at this very moment! She needs prayer. She has bad days. She weeps. She laughs. I don't spend my days twiddling my thumbs wondering what she looks like, because I know that God's plan is perfect and will be amazing, in His time. When I can put my future spouse in that perspective and leave her in God's hands, it is a joy to be faithful in my attitudes, thoughts, actions, and relationships with other members of the opposite sex.

BEN, AGE 22

fled for their lives. But the arrows of the king were swift and every one found its target. Not a single suitor vengeance of the king that day.

Penelope ran to her hero and embraced him. Then with the voice of an angel she said, "I have faithfully kept your kingdom, my noble king!" She tenderly presented him with a soft white linen roll. "I have spent years weaving this gift in hopes of your return. On the day I finished it, I was told to choose a husband." Then, placing a tender kiss upon his soiled cheek, she said, "And I choose *you*."[1]

A Hurried Generation

Isn't faithfulness heroic? Too bad our society doesn't honor it as people used to. If Penelope were a woman of today, she would have run off with the first cute prince who stepped foot on her shore. Instead, she seemed to understand what it means to guard a kingdom and wait unwaveringly for true love.

In our microwavable, fast-food generation, all our desires can be met with the click of a button. Telling you to *wait* and actually having you listen is just as likely as my throwing a side of beef to a ravenous lion and convincing him to put it in a Tupperware container and save it for tomorrow. We are used to getting everything we want *now*, and to be honest, we don't want to wait.

In fact, our generation suffers from a mental disease that my good friend Dave calls the "let-me-laugh-now-and-I'll-do-my-crying-later-if-I'm-still-alive" syndrome. In other words, most of us don't think about our future and how our decisions today will affect us over the long haul.

In my teens, I honestly never thought I would live past the age of twenty-five. Why? I don't quite know, but maybe it had something to do with the fact that I was told over 3,709 times that the end of the world was upon us. When suntanning on the beach, I drenched myself in baby oil because I just knew I wouldn't be around to suffer the consequences of skin cancer. When heating up macaroni and cheese, I would stare into the microwave like a Peeping Tom because I was certain I wouldn't be around to suffer the consequences of a warped and radiated brain. And in relationships, I would do things physically with girls that I knew were dishonoring to my future spouse because I was certain I wouldn't get married before the end of the world came.

Some have even described today's young people as "the first generation to live after the death of God." Here we are searching for something beautiful, yet the whole source of beauty has been robbed from us. The amazing and romantic world around us is explained away as a freak act of nature—our dearest friends are really only heaps of meaningless matter that evolved from a puddle of sludge. And love itself is but a chemical reaction inside our brains that takes place when our impulse to propagate the species kicks into gear.

To be honest, if modern science is right and all that exists is nothing but the result of a great big bang, then I would be the first to say that you are crazy if you *wait* to indulge your desires. I mean, if you and the "love of your life" are only heaps of meaningless matter, then hurry up and ignite that chemical reaction!

Most of us are experts in the biology, but we are illiterate when it comes to the beautiful. We tirelessly search for it, but we will never find it until we realize that the beautiful only comes from God. No matter how many times we have sex, no matter how many times we hear the words "I love you," it will forever be empty if it isn't connected with the God who invented true love and is Himself the Author of romance. When you take God out of the center of your world, everything sweet, tender, pure, and lovely is sure to quickly follow.

A Voice Crying in the Wilderness

We've been trained to be in a hurry. We pace in front of microwaves, we complain about slow service at drive-through windows, and we tap our foot impatiently for the elevator to finally arrive at the third floor. But in our minds, it's all for a good reason. We believe deep down inside that it's all coming to an end soon, and our time to indulge ourselves is rapidly decreasing every day, every minute!

But the Word of God teaches a message of purposeful patience and dazzling faithfulness. It's a message that says:

Be still, and know that I am God. (Psalm 46:10, NKJV)

In repentance and rest you will be saved, in quietness and trust is your strength. (Isaiah 30:15, NASB)

He wants to lift you up onto His lap, wrap His big strong arms around you, wipe away your tears of longing and pain, and whisper in your ear, "It's all right, little child. Just rest your head on My shoulder. I will take care of you. This world is always in a hurry, but I teach

Patience is more than endurance. A saint's life is in the hands of God like a bow and arrow in the hands of an archer. God is aiming at something the saint cannot see, and He stretches and strains, and every now and again the saint says—"I cannot stand any more." God does not heed, He goes on stretching till His purpose is in sight, then He lets fly. Trust yourself in God's hands. Maintain your relationship to Jesus Christ by the patience of faith. "Though He slay me, yet will I wait for Him." [2]

OSWALD CHAMBERS

My children patience. Learn to trust My perfect timing so you may discover that all the pain found in waiting has a magnificent and awesome purpose."

Lonely Rainy Nights

I vividly remember a lonely rainy night in 1991. I was single and not very happy about it. In fact, I was overwhelmed by the intense desire to share my life with a young woman. I tried to pray, but all I could do was heave a sigh. I didn't know Leslie yet, and to be honest, I was starting to doubt that a future spouse for me even existed. I wrestled with God, subconsciously grabbing for the "pen" I had entrusted to Him a year earlier. If God was going to script my love story, I thought *now* would be a good time to at least let me know He had picked the characters for the drama.

I like to call them "God moments." If you have ever had one, you know exactly what I mean. He is always with us, but in a "God moment" He is there with us in an intimate and life-changing way. Just as seeing the Colorado Rocky Mountains on a map doesn't compare to seeing their awesome majesty in person, so knowing that God is *there* through academic reason doesn't compare to knowing that God is *there* through experiencing a "God moment."

In a God moment, God's Word is living—it's not just literature packaged nicely inside the cover of your Bible. And in a "God moment" Jesus is alive and powerful, not just a great historical figure stowed away in the antiquated annals of the past.

So on this lonely rainy night in 1991, right smack in the middle of my pity party, I had a God moment.

I was in my room on my knees, groaning, when God poured His version of Tabasco into my heart. I remember my heart burning with the realization of how enormous, how powerful, how capable, how merciful, how tender, and how loving God is. I remember realizing, once again, how ridiculous it was for me *not* to put my complete trust in His way of doing things. And I remember weeping with my hands over my face as I once again told God, "I'm willing to wait, Lord Jesus!"

I picked up a pen, pulled a piece of notebook paper out of my desk drawer, and began to write. With

> *The sweetest things in this world today have come to us through tears and pain.*[3]
>
> J. R. MILLER

tears still dribbling down my cheeks, I was determined to somehow tell my wife-to-be, wherever she was, that I was waiting just for her. I wrote:

I feel the rain tap on my head,

Could it be your tears? Do you need a friend?

I don't know how far, and I don't know how long.

All I know is that He's faithful.

Such a love, it burns deep inside.

I know that you'll be worth all the tears that I have cried.

Years later, I pulled those simplistic words from my journal and sat down at the piano, but this time I wasn't alone. I sang to my brand-new wife the words that were crafted just for her amid my lonely, rainy night of pain-filled waiting.

Pulling a Penelope

All the chiefs and princes of the land are trying to convince us that we need to settle for less, that our hopes and dreams are unrealistic and ridiculous. But let's be faithful despite all the talk; let's patiently endure despite the fact that days, weeks, months, even years are passing by and there is still no word from our lover. Let's pull a Penelope and bring heroism back to our generation. Let's pull a Penelope and discover the stupendous and marvelous reward to patience. Let's pull a Penelope and endure the great pain to find the great gain.

Each of us will face lonely, rainy days in our lives. But very few of us know how to turn our cloudy days into a beautiful tomorrow. One of my favorite little corny sayings comes from an anniversary card Leslie and I once received. It says, "When two people really, really love each other, even rainy days are fun!"

That can be true *before* marriage, just as it can be true after those wedding bells ring. When you find yourself alone on a rainy day, pull a Penelope and weave for your future lover your own version of a white linen roll.

Most people never realize that loneliness is a gift from God. Not only can it draw us closer to Jesus, it can teach us to cherish a long-awaited marriage relationship all the more. And in that loneliness, we can weave something of our own to honor the person who will make all our faithful waiting worthwhile someday.

Learn to pray for your spouse on those rainy days, asking God to mold him or her into the perfect complement to your life. Write love letters to the one who will one day claim your love. Just think, you can invite your spouse into the deepest caverns of your heart to take a peek inside the days, months, even years of your life that he or she will not have had the privilege of sharing *except* through your writing. If you

I continually bring to mind the fact that I will not be single forever and I do not want to waste this time as a single! There is no other season in life like it, where it's just me and the Lord!... Another thing I do is to pray and ask the Lord what specifically my future husband needs me to pray for right now, in this moment. Even though I don't know him, God does, and I want to pray very intentionally for him. Sometimes I hear very specific things and sometimes I don't, so I just pray about more general things for him. Either way, mountains get moved in the spirit.

LAUREN, AGE 24

are musical, write a love song. If you're an artist, paint a picture. And if you're a woodworker, carve something that declares your conviction that your future spouse is "worth the wait"!

Believe it or not, Penelope wasn't the first to "pull a Penelope." God invented the concept of faithfulness before the beginning of time. He was the ultimate model of pain-filled patience and purposeful waiting. With tears in His tender eyes, *even now* He waits for some of us to finally let Him have His way in our life. When at last you arrive at His open palace gate, He will run to you and embrace you and whisper in your ear, "You, my child, were worth the pain-filled wait!"

> I will look to the LORD; I will wait for the God of my salvation.
>
> MICAH 7:7

> But let patience have its perfect work, that you may be perfect and complete, lacking nothing.
>
> JAMES 1:4

> My times are in Your hand.
>
> PSALM 31:15

A Look Inside Your Heart

1. In what ways has the fear of being alone impacted your approach to romantic relationships?
2. Do you really believe that if you wait for God's best, He will bring you someone worth waiting for? If not, why? If so, what is your belief based on?

3. If God has not yet brought your future spouse into your life, what purpose might He have for this time of waiting? In what areas can you be made stronger and more like Him by learning patience?

4. What tangible gifts can you "weave" now for your future spouse to reflect your commitment to waiting faithfully?

A Step Further

Hebrews 12:1–3 (NASB) provides a helpful reminder of all that Christ endured in order to set you free and give you life. As you read this passage, meditate on and thank God for all the things He has done "so that you will not grow weary and lose heart." Ask Him to infuse you with supernatural strength and a love that "bears all things, believes all things, hopes all things, [and] endures all things" (1 Corinthians 13:7). Rather than complaining to Him about your impatience to get married, you can choose instead to rejoice in this time of waiting and preparation that He is walking you through. One way to do this is to write down all the ways God is blessing your life right now and all the things you are thankful for. Then ask Him to grant you grace not to merely endure but to actually *enjoy* this unique season of your life. Remember, this life is not about you; it's about Him. And when you are so caught up in Him that He is your moment-by-moment, intimate heart-friend, loneliness becomes a thing of the past. ✕

Nine

Can the Sweeter Song Be a Solo?

The pain and purpose of singleness

✕ LESLIE ✕

Eric's face was alight with boyish excitement as he reached into his suitcase and pulled out a huge spiral notebook.

"I have something to show you, Les!" He could barely contain his enthusiasm.

It was our honeymoon—by far the most incredible two weeks of my life. After waiting for what had seemed like an eternity, we were finally married. And just when I thought I had discovered the depth of Eric's love for me, he took it to yet a deeper level.

"See all these letters?" he said, flipping through page after page of notebook paper. "I wrote these to you years before we ever met. I've been saving them for our honeymoon!"

For hours, I pored over the letters, fascinated by this man I had married. I was intrigued by his amazing journey as a single person, before I had known him.

"Tonight I am on a mission trip in Bulgaria," read one, "and I long for you to be with me in the joy of ministering God's truth."

"I am gazing at a gorgeous sunset," said another, "and it's not the same without you here to share it. I don't know where you are tonight, but I'm praying for you. I love you."

Though the letters were not addressed to me, they may as well have had my name on them. Each one, in its unique way, told of Eric's unfailing love and devotion to the woman who would one day share life with him. His faithfulness to me before we met gave me such security in our marriage. As I read the letters, I felt more like a princess than I ever thought possible. What an honor to be chosen by God to be that special woman to love this man for a lifetime!

It may seem strange that I would begin a chapter on singleness with a story of my incredible honeymoon. No, I am not trying to be cruel. This is not just a chapter about being single. This is a chapter about being single *with a purpose.* Whenever God takes us through a challenging time, we can endure the pain if we cling to the hope that in the end we will discover that it was all for a purpose, just as Christ "for the joy that was set before Him endured the cross" (Hebrews 12:2). We can know that someday it will all be worth it. Whether your singleness ends with a romantic dream come true here on this earth or a glorious celebration in eternity, God *does* have an ultimate purpose in mind for this solo season of your life.

When Eric was finally able to share those letters with me, he realized, *This was worth all those years of waiting. This was worth all those lonely, rainy nights.* And one day you, too, will be able to echo his words.

The Struggles of Singleness

"If I hear one more married person preach about singleness being a gift, I'm going to smack them!" declared Brice, a twenty-eight-year-old single we met at a speaking event in Texas. Brice is more than ready for marriage. "Married people forget what it's like to be alone!"

Maybe married people don't forget—they just block out the memory of singleness because they don't want to relive it! Singleness can be a lonely path, especially if your heart's desire is to be married. But does it have to be a form of hell on earth?

Brice has lived the past eight years in misery. He is obsessed with finding the right girl and finally shedding the "curse" of singleness. In many ways, he has put his life on hold until the issue of getting married is resolved. He hasn't tried to identify his life's calling or goals because he feels incomplete. He hasn't used this time to grow spiritually or prepare practically; he has just angrily cried out to God to send a wife to him ASAP! Brice has grown bitter and resentful. His greatest fear is dying before he finds someone to love.

Brice represents the plight of many singles in today's culture. As a Christian community, we have not acknowledged God's purpose for the season of singleness, and this is causing singles to feel devalued or "lesser than."

Jen, a fun-loving and deeply spiritual senior in college, says it seems everywhere she goes she is asked the same question: "So, are you dating anyone?"

"It's really hard to hear that question over and over," admits Jen, "because there is so much more to who I am than a relationship. I have school, ministry, and most important, my relationship with the

Lord. I hardly ever get asked about those other areas of my life; and if I do, it's only secondary to people wanting to find out about the relationship area. When the focus is so much on relationships, it's easy to start thinking that you need to have a relationship to be considered a whole person. But that's not true. I am a whole person right now, even in this season of singleness."

The fact that Jen understands there is so much more to her life than just finding a relationship is truly remarkable in a culture that puts so much emphasis on the importance of pairing up with someone. She has had just as much indirect pressure from Christians in her life to find someone as from non-Christians. She feels a lack of support from the body of Christ in her commitment to trust God for her future spouse.

Countless other young women I've met are basically just waiting around for their future spouse. They don't feel their lives can really begin until they are married. A common joke on college campuses is,

Even if I never marry, I'm content with being single, for He has truly given me a joyful life that has been filled with so many rich spiritual experiences and opportunities. I wouldn't trade these years that God has given me "set-apart-in-singleness" for anything! Singleness is not something God gave me in one big lump sum and said, "Here, swallow this!" If He had, I probably couldn't have handled it. But it's been a process…learning to be faithful, to be patient, to save my heart, and to wait on Him, one day, one year, one season at a time!

MEL, AGE 31

"Oh, she's here to get her M.R.S. degree." In other words, she could care less about college; she just wants to find a husband!

In spite of the temptation to wait for life to begin until after we find the person we are going to marry, God does have more in mind for us during a season of singleness than just learning the art of misery and impatience.

Radiant Singleness: Krissy's Story

Eric's older sister, Krissy, decided from a very young age to live a life of faithfulness to her future husband. As she entered her twenties, she had never been in a relationship. Guys had shown interest, but Krissy was holding out for a man whose life was completely centered around Jesus Christ, a man who would not merely appreciate her personality and outward appearance but would be drawn to her because of a mutual passion for Jesus Christ.

Though she deeply desired to be married and raise a family, Krissy lived her single years entirely focused on Jesus Christ. No matter where she was, she poured out her life for Him, loving and serving everyone around her. She didn't put off living until she finally met her future husband; instead, she lived fully and radiantly each and every day, drawing rich fulfillment and joy from her passionate romance with Jesus Christ.

Krissy was (and is) an attractive woman. But she wasn't obsessed with making herself more appealing to the opposite sex. Rather, she was consumed with her heavenly Prince. The only applause that mattered to her was His. Instead of trying to conform to the world's ideals, she spent her time and energy living out the gospel of Christ: serving the poor, teaching small children, going into the mission field, and sharing Christ with hurting people. During all of her single years, though there were certainly times of loneliness, Krissy was not consumed with discontentment or self-pity, but with Jesus Christ alone.

When Krissy was in her late twenties and still with no prospects for marriage, her younger brother Mark asked her one day if she was "called to singleness." She pondered the question for a minute, then replied, "Today I am." What an incredible response! She knew that no matter what God had planned for her future, He would give her the grace she needed to live as a radiant, fulfilled, Christ-honoring single woman *today.* She didn't worry about being single for the next twenty years; she simply trusted God for the grace to be single one day at a time.

As she entered her thirties, people began to pressure Krissy to try to snag a guy while she still could. "You should move to a big city where there are more available men," some suggested. "Why don't you start trying a little harder to get guys' attention?" others urged. It was tempting to listen to these well-meaning words. She wasn't getting any younger, and she longed for an earthly love story. Most of the godly men she met were already married. What if she never met anyone? What if she never got married? But the gentle words of her Prince resonated through her soul, "Am I enough?" Even if He never brought a man into her life, Krissy resolved to remain fully set apart for Him. Jesus Christ, not the hope of an earthly romance, was the focus of her existence and the source of her fulfillment.

One day, as Krissy was teaching a Bible study, a young man named

Scott walked into the room. He was thirty-six years old, and had never given his heart to a woman. He'd been faithfully holding out for a Christlike princess all of his life. As he listened to Krissy speak passionately about Jesus Christ, Scott was intrigued. Her eyes shone and her face glowed as she spoke about the Lover of her soul. She seemed completely unconcerned that her overwhelming passion for Christ might make her look or sound foolish to the world. He'd never seen a woman who sparkled with such radiance, such all-consuming love for her Lord.

Scott came back the next week. And the week after that. Soon, he and Krissy became good friends, drawn together by their mutual love for Christ. And the more he observed of her life, the more fascinated he became. She wasn't like other girls—even other Christian girls. She never changed her personality around him or tried to draw attention to herself. She was far more focused on Christ than on trying to turn his head or win his heart.

Krissy possessed a spectacular inner glow that enchanted Scott. The longer he was around her, the more he was drawn to Jesus Christ. After a two-year friendship, Scott asked Krissy to marry him. After much prayer, she said yes. Their friendship and romance was beautiful, tender, sweet, and pure—with Christ always at the center. I was recruited to sing at their wedding as Krissy walked down the aisle. As the guests took their seats, the music began and I started my song. But the moment she entered the room in her white wedding dress, radiant and glowing, my throat closed with emotion. No sound would come. (It didn't help that I could see Eric in the front row, his face contorted with sobs!) The room was flooded with the brilliant presence of God. I could almost see Christ standing there applauding, His eyes beaming with love and tears of joy glistening on His face as He watched His precious princess walk down the aisle, a sparklingly pure bride. Krissy had remained faithful and set apart for Him and for her future husband since the age of twelve. And today she was receiving His blessing, His reward.

That wedding was the most amazing, tender, and supernaturally beautiful ceremony I have ever seen—including my own, which, in my humble opinion, is a very close second! Today, Scott and Krissy have three adorable children—a girl and two boys. Her dream of having a family has come true. And yet the foundation of her existence is still her passionate ongoing romance with Jesus Christ. He is still her first love and the Lord of her life. And her stunning beauty comes from His radiant life within her.

Not without design does God write the music of our lives. Be it ours to learn the tune, and not be dismayed at the "rests." They are not to be slurred over, not to be omitted, not to destroy the melody, not to change the keynote. If we look up, God Himself will beat the time for us. With the eye on Him, we shall strike the next note full and clear. If we sadly say to ourselves, "There is no music in a 'rest,'" let us not forget "there is the making of music in it." The making of music is often a slow and painful process in this life. How patiently God works to teach us! How long He waits for us to learn the lesson![1]

JOHN RUSKIN

Is He Enough?

Before Eric came into my life, I was attempting to wait faithfully for my future husband and set my life apart for him in mind, heart, and body. But at times, loneliness and impatience clouded my perspective. I sometimes lost sight of the fact that I was living in purity as an act of love for my King, not just so that I could reap the reward of a God-written love story. In these moments I bought into the lie that the only way I could be truly happy or fulfilled was if God brought "the one" into my life. The greatest desire of my heart was to be married. One day a friend encouraged me with Psalm 37:4: "Delight yourself in the LORD; and He will give you the desires of your heart" (NASB).

As I meditated on those words, an awakening began to dawn upon my soul. My dream of a beautiful love story could not take over first place in my heart. Unless Christ Himself became my truest delight and my all in all, He could not fulfill the desires of my heart. He needed to train me to truly delight in Him, to find my deepest satisfaction in Him alone. Then He would *shape* the desires of my heart to match His dreams and plans for my life. As I wrote in *Authentic Beauty*:

> The reality is that the only way to discover the true beauty of
> a God-written love story with another person on this earth
> is to delight in Jesus Christ with all our heart, soul, mind,
> and strength—to find our security and joy in Him alone.
> Rather than focus all our efforts on the pursuit of a human
> relationship, we must center our life on the pursuit of intimacy

with our true Prince. Only out of intimacy with our heavenly Lover can the beauty of a God-written human love story be experienced.[2]

Often God will delay bringing an earthly love story into our life until we have truly given Him first place in our heart. Intimacy with Him must be enough to satisfy our deepest longings, even if a human romance never comes into our life. Even after marriage, we cannot look to our spouse to fulfill needs that only Christ can meet. If we do, we'll inevitably be disillusioned and disappointed. An earthly romance can never take the place of an intimate relationship with Christ. If we lean on a human love story as our primary source of fulfillment and happiness, we'll never find what we are looking for. But when we find our fulfillment in Jesus Christ, we are free to selflessly love our spouse instead of constantly thinking about our own needs and wants.

When I allow Christ to be my joy, peace, and security, my relationship with Eric radically changes. Instead of always worrying about whether Eric is meeting *my* needs or fulfilling *my* romantic ideals, I am able to focus on serving him and giving to him. The secret to a marriage thriving for a lifetime is *selflessness*. Nothing will kill a marriage faster than two people who are only concerned with meeting their own needs and desires. But nothing nurtures romance and beauty into blossom like two people who put each other's needs and desires above their own. Eric has truly been shaped into a heroic prince and husband. He grows more sensitive toward me and more romantic as the years go by. But it's not because I drop hints, criticize, or complain. It's because I allow my intimate relationship with Jesus Christ to fulfill the deepest desires of my heart rather than putting that burden upon my husband's shoulders.

Long before God brings your spouse into your life, you can set the stage for a spectacular marriage by learning to find all your joy and fulfillment in Him alone. Even after marriage, there are no guarantees that you'll always have your spouse by your side, able to love and serve you. Remember Karen and Scott's story? Scott is no longer able to be the strong, capable husband Karen married. If Karen didn't find her fulfillment in Christ, she would be miserable and full of self-pity. Instead, she overflows with joy and contentment, and her marriage is a testimony of the breathtaking love of Christ.

Richard and Sabina Wurmbrand, a pastor and his wife who lived in Romania when the Soviets invaded, had one of the most beautiful love stories I've ever heard. Ironically, their marriage wasn't the fairy-tale ideal that most of us dream about. Because of their commitment to Christ, under the Communist regime they both were thrown into prison, tortured, impoverished, and separated from each other for more than ten years, not knowing if the other person was dead or alive. Yet their flame of love never dwindled. When they were finally reunited, they were sickly, starving, and carrying lasting scars from abuse. But they remained passionately in love. Even without all of the things that typically make a romance beautiful, Richard and Sabina discovered a depth of love that few couples ever find. Why? Because Jesus Christ was their first love. They loved each other dearly—but they loved Jesus Christ more. And even through extreme hardship, heartache, and separation, their love did not fail, because *He was enough.*

"Am I enough?" came the gentle challenge of my Prince, and His tender voice drowned out all the clamoring confusion in my mind. Jesus was, and would always be, much more than enough. He did not desire to destroy my life, to leave me as a desolate, lonely failure alone in the woods somewhere. He wanted me to put Him first, above everything else—to give my heart, time, affection, energy, and devotion to Him alone. He gently assured me that as I pursued Him and Him alone, all my other needs would be met. In the meantime, my only concern must be to worship Him with every fiber of my being.[3]

LESLIE LUDY, *AUTHENTIC BEAUTY*

Will you, too, allow Jesus Christ to become your all in all, the Lover of your soul, the delight of your heart? If so, whether or not you ever get married, you will experience intimacy, romance, and true love in all of its glory and splendor.

If You Are Lonely...

Eric endured a period of profound loneliness while he was taking a semester off from college. He had just come from a busy schedule at school that included sports, study, and an active social life. Now, back at home with an empty schedule while all his buddies were still at school and his family was occupied with their own lives, he felt an intense inward pain like nothing he'd ever before known. One day he found himself on his knees, weeping into the fabric of the sofa. The loneliness had become too much to handle. As he cried out to his Lord, he suddenly felt a tremendous peace wash over him. It was almost as if Jesus Himself were kneeling beside Eric, wrapping a tender arm around his shoulders and whispering words of love and comfort to his soul.

That afternoon Eric sat at the piano and wrote this song:

I am like a deer, You are like the water.
I run to You, like a son to his Father.
I felt so alone, like a moth without a flame,
But You ignited, and to You I came,
And that's forever.

I felt so alone, like a ship without a sea.
But You gave me water,
You took my hand and said to me,
"This is for eternity."

I'll never be lonely,
I'll never be lonely with You.
I've got this feeling that You're here to stay,
And I know I'll never be lonely with You.

Elisabeth Elliot once said, "Loneliness is a required course for leadership." If God is preparing you to make an impact on this world for His kingdom, chances are He will take you through a season of solitude. This is a season when you learn that you can't lean upon anyone but Him for your confidence and when you gain the strength to stand alone even when no one else stands with you.

In the past fourteen years of Christian ministry, Eric and I have often been incredibly grateful for the seasons of loneliness we experienced before we were married—those times when we learned to stand firm in our convictions and find refuge and comfort in the arms of our King, to live for only His smile, even when it seemed no one else was smiling upon us. So many times in standing for Truth we have felt utterly alone. If we hadn't allowed God to give each of us a strong backbone and prepare us to stand apart from the crowd, we surely would have crumbled and compromised a long time ago.

Don't despise loneliness. Instead, allow it to chase you into the ready arms of your King. If you turn to Him instead of trying to fill the void with other things, you will find that He is ready to meet your every need. You'll also discover that He may be using loneliness to prepare and equip you to be a leader, to stand firm when everyone else's courage is failing, and to live for the applause of your King alone.

> *Nearly all God's jewels are crystallized tears.*[4]
>
> MRS. CHARLES E. COWMAN

Fruitful Singleness

Paul says in 1 Corinthians 7 that singleness is a benefit because it enables a person to focus on serving the Lord without distraction. Those who, like Krissy, are willing to allow God to use this season of their lives for *His purposes* will discover an incredible truth: singleness doesn't have to be a time of passive and futile waiting. Instead it can be an exciting adventure of actively serving in God's kingdom, cultivating unhindered intimacy with Christ, and even practically preparing for a future marriage. If you think you'll automatically know how to be an excellent husband or wife once you walk down the aisle, think again. Just as faithfulness is an art to be cultivated long before your wedding day, so are the practical life skills that will make you a great marriage partner.

Before Eric came into my life, I had to go through a time of practical preparation for married life. I had managed to enter young adulthood without learning how to keep a budget, balance a checkbook, pay bills, or even cook real food that was not from a can or box. I had been too preoccupied with my social life and school to focus on tasks that didn't really affect my life at the time. God wanted to prepare me in some of the most basic areas I had missed *before* He brought a man into my life and things would drastically change. For about a year, my focus became practical preparation in basic life skills. And believe me, Eric is quite appreciative that I learned those things!

Being married in the real world takes teamwork. Those who are of the mind-set that they can rely on their spouse to do all the practical work of living a responsible adult life are in for a rocky relationship.

I know many guys whose mothers cooked for them, made their beds, and did their laundry until the day they left home. As a result they never learned even the most elementary aspects of keeping house. One of two scenarios usually takes place in these unfortunate men's lives. Either they become bachelors with homes that need to be quarantined by the health department, or they get married and drive their poor wives to the brink of insanity by leaving a trail of dirty socks, dishes, and open toilet seats, expecting her to take care of it. Needless to say, the first scenario doesn't add to the aura of desirability of a bachelor looking for love, and the second situation causes some fairly heated conflicts that can send couples scrambling for marriage counseling even before the honeymoon is over.

Guys, take a little advice and use this time of singleness to prepare in practical ways for managing a home. The woman you marry will love you for it, and you will significantly reduce the amount of nagging you are subject to during your married lifetime!

Eric, my noble knight, is usually the one who cleans the bathroom in our house (something I can't stand doing). Whenever he selflessly scrubs the toilet without complaining, I am reminded once again how blessed I am to have a man like him. This may not sound romantic, but to me it is *very* romantic! Eric displays his undying love for me when he gives of himself in these simple, basic ways.

This advice isn't just for guys. It's for everyone. My goal is to serve Eric in everyday life, just as he serves me. While he cleans the bathroom, I do the laundry, which is the one thing *he* can't stand doing. (The unsolvable mystery of mismatched socks always frustrates him beyond words.)

Why not ask God to show you what practical areas in your life need some work? Maybe it's not housework, but learning how to budget and keep track of finances. Maybe it's learning how to grocery shop and prepare meals. Maybe it's basic manners and respect. Headsup: if you are the kind of person who belches, chews with an open mouth, emits foul odors, and goes to the bathroom with the door wide

Service to God (mission trips, ministry ventures, serving at a local church) is so fulfilling as a single person. I want to use these few years (or possibly many years) of singleness and exhaust them for God's kingdom! I believe God will bring me into a new season of service for His kingdom through marriage, but at this moment it isn't my job to wait by the phone and wait around for "the one."... I repeatedly have had to check my heart and say, "Lord, if you call me to a life of singleness then make it my joy to do Your will." As 1 John repeatedly explains, "His commands are not burdensome." Therefore, since God has commanded singleness in this season of my life, this command must have been designed by God to bring me more joy in Him.

BEN, AGE 22

open, you might want to consider adding a bit of chivalry or dignity to your habits. Basic principle: if you want a healthy sex life in marriage, don't be a cave man (or woman).

Every day that you are single can be a chance to love your future spouse by preparing for your life together. Don't waste this season, but let God help you cultivate every opportunity to become the man or woman they are dreaming of.

Marriage Is for Everyone

If you think it's hard waiting for marriage before you meet your spouse, it's even harder to wait for marriage after you meet. The longer Eric and I were engaged, the more intense our longing grew to finally be together. About two months before the wedding, we half-jokingly thought about eloping just to put ourselves out of the misery. But we knew that taking our vows in front of family and friends would be so special. Plus, it had taken me countless hours of shopping to find the perfect wedding dress. I was not going to miss my chance to show it off.

So we stuck it out. Eric was teaching in Michigan, while I remained in Colorado. We racked up quite a phone bill over those few months. I was constantly calling to remind him to make hotel reservations, invite relatives to the rehearsal dinner, and go get sized for a tux. Like a true bachelor, he waited until the last possible day to accomplish all of these tasks, but he did get them done, thankfully. And finally it was down to the last week before our wedding. Two days before Eric hopped a flight to Colorado to get married, he had to teach one last day of Constitutional Law to his students. Needless to say, his mind was anywhere but on the five key elements to the Preamble.

"All I could think about was Leslie, Leslie, Leslie," he said. "My vocabulary had been reduced to one word: *Leslie!* I couldn't teach. I couldn't carry on a normal conversation with anyone. I couldn't even pray!"

The last day of class, Eric made up a creative game for his students to play since his mind was mush anyway. Any guesses what the name of his game was? That's right. L-e-s-l-i-e. (In case you're wondering, it had nothing to do with Constitutional Law.)

For four hours he forced his poor students to play "L-e-s-l-i-e." They were probably running for the door when class was finally dismissed, convinced that their lovesick teacher had finally snapped.

But Eric didn't care. He was so excited to be married…nothing else mattered.

Back in Colorado, I was feeling the same way. The anticipation of wearing my dress and walking down the aisle was nothing compared to the longing I had to finally be with the man I loved.

And that's when we realized a profound truth. This longing to be with the one we loved was precisely the longing we should have to be with our Lord Jesus Christ, our true Bridegroom for all eternity. There's a reason Christ's welcome to those who join Him in heaven is called the "marriage supper of the Lamb" in the book of Revelation. It will be the ultimate marriage celebration: the most perfect Bridegroom of all time being united with His Bride, whom He redeemed with His own blood. Marriage is for every child of God. Whether or not we ever take marriage vows on this earth, we enter into a sacred marriage covenant with our eternal Husband the moment we give Him our life.

There is an ancient story passed down through generations of Christians about the apostle Peter during the latter years of his life. It was said that he wept whenever a cock would crow. Of course, if we know Bible history, we understand why. But it was also said that Peter often wept at other times, and no one quite knew the reason. Finally one day, a young saint worked up enough courage to ask him about it.

"Peter, why do you so often weep?" he inquired cautiously.

Peter turned to the young man, and with a look of intense yearning in his eyes, he replied softly, *"Desiderio Domini."*

Translated from Latin into modern-day English, *Desiderio Domini* means, "I dearly long to be with my Lord."

Peter had spent his time among men. Now he was ready for

Singleness is not a hindrance to living a completely fulfilled life in Jesus Christ. The apostle Paul is a stellar example of this. Whenever I feel lonely I find a quiet place to study God's Word. By praying and seeking His direction in my life, I lose all the doubts about His path for me. ...Focusing solely on Christ and His path is the only way I am absolutely content and fulfilled as a woman, single or not.

DAVINA, AGE 19

heaven, with a longing that grew stronger each and every day to be able to run into the loving arms of his dearest friend and Savior, Jesus Christ.

Your longing to be with an earthly lover may be overwhelming at times. But until your heart is consumed with love and longing for your heavenly Bridegroom, you'll miss out on the greatest love story of all time. Jesus Christ is not meant to be our stand-in until we meet our spouse. Rather, Jesus Christ *is* our spouse—our Bridegroom, our Husband, the Lover of our soul. Earthly marriage is only meant to give us a small glimpse of a much more important marriage: our heavenly marriage. Our longing to be with our future spouse should pale in comparison to our longing to be with our true Bridegroom.

Don't miss out on a divine romance because you are so caught up in finding an earthly one. Whether married or single, we all have a God-written love story to experience—and yours can start right now.

...the fullness of Him who fills all in all.

EPHESIANS 1:23

Yet indeed I also count all things loss for the excellence of the knowledge of Christ Jesus my Lord, for whom I have suffered the loss of all things, and count them as rubbish, that I may gain Christ.

PHILIPPIANS 3:8

A Look Inside Your Heart

1. Are you putting off happiness and contentment until you meet your spouse, or are you finding fulfillment right now in Christ? Explain your answer.
2. How can you use this season of your life to serve others instead of being caught up in loneliness and self-pity? What changes do you need to make in your focus, direction, and attitude in order to bring glory to Christ during your single years?
3. What practical life skills can you work at strengthening now to help prepare yourself for a healthy marriage later?
4. How would your life change if you fully and genuinely embraced Jesus as the Lover of your soul?

A Step Further

Some of God's greatest heroes were single. In fact, their singleness freed them to focus fully on their calling in God's kingdom. Take some time to study the amazing life and ministry of Paul in the book of Acts. He was single and fully satisfied in Christ. Read 1 Corinthians 7:7–8, and be reminded that singleness is a high calling, whether for a season or for a lifetime. Write a prayer of thanks to God for this season of singleness, and list specific ways in which you desire to grow and mature during this time of your life. If you trust Him, He will give you grace to fulfill your high calling with joy. ✕

Ten

Holding Out for a Fairy Tale

How high should we set our hopes?

✄ LESLIE ✄

All my life I had dreams of *him*. The ideal man. His sandy-blond hair had a wind-blown, outdoorsy look and perfectly complemented his bronzed skin. His bright blue eyes sparkled at all times, and whenever he smiled, the dimple on his chin stood out in the most adorable way.

He was a perfect gentleman. The ideal blend of strength and sensitivity. The kind of guy who could beat up twenty bad guys with one hand and offer me a dozen red roses with the other.

Maybe it came from an overdose of Barbie and *Cinderella* when I was young. I always imagined that I would marry a guy who was a perfect blend of Prince Charming from *Cinderella* (or maybe the prince from *Snow White*—I think they might possibly be the same guy) and Ken (as in Ken and Barbie).

At any rate, my standards were just a little high when I entered the dating world. I was always on the lookout for this man of my dreams. I had no doubt that he would show himself soon and carry me away to his castle.

This presented a problem. Not only were there absolutely no guys who fit the description, but they all seemed to be the exact *opposite* of what I was looking for. I was in search of a gorgeous knight in shining armor, and all I saw around me were a bunch of egotistical, selfish, sex-obsessed, immature slobs who didn't even know what the word *gentleman* meant.

One of my first wake-up calls came when I was only fourteen. I was talking on the phone with one of my guy friends. After about an hour of discussing innocuous topics such as math homework, music, and movies, we ran out of things to say. There was an unspoken rule among fourteen-year-olds that you had to get in at least five hours of phone talking each night. (This was long before the days of IMing, texting, and the like.) I was still about two hours short of quota, and so was he. Hanging up the phone and doing our homework was simply not an option. As we pondered our dilemma, he had a brainstorm.

"I know!" he said. "Kyle is over at Trevor's house right now. Let me call them up on three-way, and I won't tell them you're listening in. Then you can hear what a guy conversation sounds like when girls aren't around!"

Naively, I thought his idea was brilliant and waited enthusiastically while he dialed up Trevor's phone number. Within moments, the three of them were bantering back and forth in their crackly monotones, the way only fourteen-year-old guys can. At first I was bored with their discussion about weightlifting and trying out for the basketball team, but then they moved on to a topic that instantly caught my attention: girls.

I held my breath as I waited for them to reveal their true feelings about the girls they liked. But the words they spoke were not what I was expecting. They began describing, in perverse and graphic detail, exactly what they liked about the bodies of girls from school and what they wanted to do with them sexually. They talked about the female anatomy as if girls were nothing more than pieces of meat to devour. It was like I was listening to a porn show, but worse, because the girls they were talking about were my friends.

Soon my guy friend hung up with his buddies (guys' conversations never seem to last as long as girls') and asked me, "So what did you think of that?"

"Is that how you guys always talk about girls?" I asked a bit incredulously.

"Sure. Why?"

"So you guys basically see girls as sex objects?" I questioned, trying to keep the anger out of my voice.

"Well, sort of, yeah," was his brutally honest response.

That was my first indication that finding a knight in shining armor was not going to be as easy as I had always imagined. As I grew older, I decided that if I wanted to experience dating relationships like everyone else, I was going to have to lower my standards of what I wanted in a guy. Over the next few years, I went from dreaming of a noble and perfect Prince Charming to settling for any guy who seemed remotely interested in me.

Even after I stepped away from temporary dating relationships and made the decision to set my life apart for my future husband, there were times when my commitment to purity felt useless. I suffered through quite a long season before God brought a handful of godly guy friends I could actually respect into my life. And until I met them, I often wondered if waiting for something beyond the warped manhood of the culture would even prove worthwhile. What was the point of aspiring to the "sweeter song," of trusting God for a beautiful romance, of setting myself aside in selfless love for my future spouse, if men worth waiting for didn't even exist?

Countless young women ask this question every day. But ironically, it's not just young women who want to know if they'll ever find someone worth waiting for. Eric and I have met hundreds of guys who wonder if there are any set-apart girls left in the world.

I remember having a conversation with a friend of mine who had been married to a wonderful Christian man for five years. "I don't know if my standards are too high," I told her. "I am so confused. I have all these desires for a certain type of man, but I haven't seen even one guy who fits what I'm longing for in a husband."

"Leslie, what are the main qualities you've always wanted in a man?" she asked in reply.

I thought for a moment, then whipped out the mental checklist I'd tucked away in a corner of my mind, adding to it over the years. "Well, I want someone who is completely focused on Christ, someone who treats me like a princess, someone who is sensitive, strong, full of integrity, servant-hearted, and loves kids." Then I laughed at how ridiculous it all sounded. "I guess I'm holding out for Prince Charming," I admitted.

"Not really," she replied. "Just think about all those qualities you mentioned. Who can you think of that is the perfect example of all those character traits?"

"Uh…Superman?" (I'd had a thing for Clark Kent since fourth grade.)

"No. Jesus Christ," she responded. "The desires you have for that kind of man have been in your heart from a young age. But you are not the one who came up with those longings. It was God who put them in your heart, because He wants you to look for a man who is like Jesus Christ."

It was an incredible realization. *God* had given me the desire for a godly, Christlike man because that's exactly the type of man He wanted to bring me. It wasn't that I was supposed to hold out for a man who never made mistakes and was absolutely perfect in every way. Maybe my childhood imaginings had been a bit larger than life. It was probably a bit frivolous to hold out for a Ken doll look-alike with sandy-blond hair and bronzed skin. But in no way did God want me to settle for one of the typical selfish jerks who were a dime a dozen. He wanted me to save myself for a man who exhibited His very nature and character. And He wanted me to trust Him enough to bring that guy to me in His perfect time.

And guess what? In His perfect time, that's exactly what He did. Eric is my valiant, strong, sensitive knight in shining armor. He is far more than I ever hoped for or desired in a man. Daily I thank God I didn't settle for less than His best for me.

Too many women become desperate. They are hungry for attention and affection, so they settle for guys who don't know the first thing about how to treat a woman. They are impatient—they don't trust that God could have something better for them. So they compromise. They give themselves to men who really aren't worth a second glance.

Christlike men who have learned to treat women with dignity and respect are rare. Even guys who hang out at church and strum praise songs on their guitars often fall short of Christ's standards. Too many Christian men have patterned their actions toward the female sex after the woman-conquering men of Hollywood rather than after the woman-honoring Jesus Christ.

Likewise, too many men stop waiting for a truly set-apart young woman. Few girls in today's world could be characterized as a princess of purity—a woman who is fully set apart in body, heart, and mind for her husband. When Eric was in college, he often felt like there were no girls left on the planet who were saving themselves physically, let alone emotionally, for their future husbands. The only exception was his older sister, Krissy. He had to believe that if God had someone like Krissy set aside for a man, then somewhere else in the world God was molding another woman with that same kind of purity for him.

The sad reality is that most modern women are manipulative, flirtatious, and self-focused when relating to men. They play games with guys' hearts. They trade their priceless pearl of purity for temporary pleasure. While it may be hard for a girl to believe that a Christlike knight exists, it's equally difficult for a man of integrity to trust God for a set-apart woman.

But only those who refuse to lower their standards reap the purest rewards.

The godly young men I've spoken with believe that if young women started keeping their standards high rather than settling for mediocre men, guys would be forced to make serious changes to their masculinity. And even if you are mocked, ridiculed, or ignored because of your stand, you can be sure that God will honor your decision. He paid for the treasure of your heart with His own blood. You disregard His amazing sacrifice for you when you allow your femininity to be trampled in the mud. You are a daughter of the King, so hold out for a man who has royal blood coursing through his veins.[1]

LESLIE LUDY, *ANSWERING THE GUY QUESTIONS*

A True Love Story

Lieutenant John Blandford was in New York City at Grand Central station, and he looked up at the big clock. It said five till six. His heart was racing. At exactly six o'clock he was going to meet the girl whom he thought he was in love with but had never met. This is what had happened…

While he was in training as a fighter pilot during World War II, he happened to go to a library and checked out a book. As he flipped through the pages, he noticed that someone had made notes in the margins. Reading the insightful observations in beautiful handwriting, he said to himself, *I would love to meet whoever wrote these notes; they seem so kind, gentle, and wise.*

He looked in the front of the book and saw a name: Hollis

Meynell, New York City. He decided to try to find her. With the help of a New York City phone book, he found her address and wrote her a letter. The day after he wrote her, he was shipped overseas to fight in the war.

Surprisingly, Hollis answered John's letter. The two corresponded back and forth throughout the war. "Her letters were just like the marvelous notes she had written in that book," John recalled. "She was so comforting and so helping."

One time John had confessed in a letter that he had been scared to death when he'd found himself surrounded by enemy planes. Hollis had assured him that all brave men are afraid at times. She suggested that the next time he felt fear, he should imagine her voice reciting, "Yea, though I walk through the valley of the shadow of death, I will fear no evil, for Thou art with me."

As they continued to write, John began to realize that he was having romantic feelings toward Hollis. He wrote, "Send me a picture," and she declined saying, "If your feeling for me has any reality, what I look like won't matter."

Still, he was intrigued by this woman and longed to meet her in person. Finally the day came when he was to return to the States on leave. He mentioned in one of his letters that he was coming home and would like to take her to dinner. She arranged to meet him in Grand Central station at 6:00 p.m. by the big clock. "You'll know who I am because I'll be wearing a red rose," she wrote.

At last the day had come. John waited nervously to finally meet the girl he thought he loved. Then his heart leaped as a young woman approached, her slim figure capped off by an attractive face framed with curling blond hair. In her pale-green suit she looked fresh and lively, and her flower-blue eyes sparkled.

He moved toward her without realizing she was *not* wearing a rose. She welcomed his approach with a quiet, "Going my way, soldier?" But as he took another step, he realized that just beyond her stood another woman—a plump, graying woman with a red rose adorning her rumpled coat.

He stopped cold, utterly torn between following the winsome young beauty in the green suit and keeping his commitment to the woman whose letters had so uplifted him during the war.

Abruptly, he made his decision. With unhesitating strides he approached the plump woman, whose face beamed with a warm smile. "I'm Lieutenant John Blandford, and you—you must be Miss Meynell. I'm so glad you could meet me. Would you join me for dinner?"

The woman's smile grew broader with what appeared to be quiet amusement. "I don't know what this is all about, Son," she said. Then she pointed toward a figure in a green suit, who was now nearly out of sight. "That young lady gave me this rose and asked me to wear it while walking through the train station. She said that if you asked me to go with you, I was to let you know she'd be waiting for you in the restaurant across the street.

"She said it was some kind of a test."[2]

Going for the Gold

The extraordinary and romantic story of John Blandford and Hollis Meynell is an incredible example of a young woman who was willing to wait for a man with true integrity—and a man who was rewarded because he did not follow his fleshly desires but responded with the character of Christ.

To experience a God-written love story, our standards for what we are seeking in a relationship *cannot* be determined by our culture. Our standards should be radically higher than the rest of the world's. No, we shouldn't expect perfection in a future spouse. But we *should* expect to see the attitude of Christ reflected in that person's life.

Guys, learn to follow the example of the Perfect Gentleman, Jesus Christ, in how you treat women. If you do, you'll stand head and shoulders above the typical jerks of today and be worthy of a beautiful princess of purity who is saving herself just for you.

Girls, if you will wait patiently and confidently for God to bring a Christlike man into your life, you will not be disappointed. Important side note: I've had many single women respond to this statement in frustration over the years, telling me, "I've waited and waited for a godly guy. I've kept my standards high. But the only thing that's happened is that all the available men got married and I'm still alone. I should have gotten married when I had the chance." Don't buy into that lie. Why would you lower your standards just to avoid singleness? Being married to a self-serving, ungodly guy is far worse than being alone; just ask any woman whose life is now in shambles because she made the mistake of marrying a jerk. A love story that is humanly scripted rather than divinely orchestrated isn't worth the pain and heartache that will surely come as a result of taking matters into your own hands. Jesus Christ purchased you with His very own blood. He is far too jealous over your life to give you to just any Joe Blow who looks your way. His protection is not something to resent but to rejoice in!

How God's heart must break when, because of our foolishness, we miss the beautiful things He has planned.

I recently read of a youth pastor who counseled a distraught young woman about a relationship she was in. This young girl was head over heels in love with a certain young man. They had been dating a few weeks, and the young man had started pressuring her to have sex with him and compromise her standards.

"What should I do?" she asked the youth pastor. "I like him so much. I don't want to lose him."

The youth pastor told

I determined at a young age what I was looking for in a man spiritually and character-wise, and I made a list of the "uncompromisables." That list still stands. And it has helped me keep my head on straight on more than one occasion! Just because the man does take the lead and some things look good, if other "character essentials" aren't there, I don't just fall for the first knight that comes riding by.

MEL, AGE 31

her to simply be firm with the young man and tell him that if the relationship was going to continue, she could not be pressured to compromise her standards in the area of purity.

"It took a while for the message to sink in to the young man's head," the youth pastor proudly recalled, "but finally he realized where she stood and he respected her. They were able to enjoy a normal, healthy dating relationship without her being pressured to give away her virginity, though she had to continually remind him of her standards."

If this young girl had come to me for advice, I would have said something along these lines: "This guy isn't worth a second look. True manhood doesn't seek to compromise a woman's purity. True manhood stands up to heroically protect it. Don't throw your life away on a self-focused guy just because you're attracted to him. You are worth far more to God than that, and He has something far better planned for your life. Trust God enough to let Him bring a *real* man into your life, one who will care as much about protecting your sacred purity as you do."

Of course, God doesn't want us to hold out for someone who never makes mistakes. But He does want us to hold out for a guy or girl who is far more focused on Jesus Christ than on fulfilling a selfish personal agenda. Keeping your standards high comes down to an issue of trust. Do you really trust God to bring someone into your life, or do you feel the need to manipulate and take matters into your own hands? Remember that He knows your deepest dreams and desires even more than you do. And He delights to give good and perfect gifts to His children. But we must be patient and let Him do it in His own perfect time and way. Beware of rushing ahead of God and taking the pen back into your own hands even after you have supposedly surrendered it to Him.

Remember Krissy's story? God brought a godly man into her life when she wasn't even looking for one. Krissy didn't find her husband through frantic searches on Internet dating sites, carefully schemed visits to singles' mixers, or a frenzy of short-term flings. Scott came into Krissy's life without any human manipulation. Krissy simply trusted in her faithful King with all of her heart and built her life around doing His work—and He took care of the rest.

Every couple Eric and I have met who has truly experienced a God-scripted love story shares a similar experience. They literally came into each other's lives out of nowhere, without human strategy or manipulation. They put all of their trust in their Lord, and He proved faithful beyond all their hopes and expectations.

We serve a big God. It's time to start believing He is capable of bringing a marriage partner into your life in His own perfect, miraculous way—and that He doesn't need your help. He doesn't need your fumbling fingers grabbing the pen back out of His hand and trying to script your own story.

If our hopes are being disappointed just now, it means that they are being purified. There is nothing noble the human mind has ever hoped for or dreamed of that will not be fulfilled. One of the greatest strains in life is the strain of waiting for God. "Because thou hast kept the word of my patience." Remain spiritually tenacious.[3]

OSWALD CHAMBERS

This doesn't mean you remain passive in the process. But your role is not to frantically search for a spouse and then ask God to bless your selfishly motivated decisions. Rather, your role is to pray, to trust, to build your life around Him, to listen to His still, small voice of guidance…and let Him take care of the rest.

If you desire a beautiful God-written love story, your time will be far better spent cultivating your relationship with Christ than searching the Internet or the local coffee shops for good-looking potentials. If you really learn to trust Him, understand His heart, and recognize His voice, then you will be able to *recognize* His fingerprints when He begins to write your love story.

Don't ever forget who your God is. He is the One who valued you so much that He sent His only Son to die that you might be redeemed. He has amazing things in store for those who trust Him. And as the well-known saying goes, "God gives His best to those who leave the choice to Him." Next time you are tempted to rush ahead of God and lower your standards, remember the words of Paul: "He who did not spare His own Son, but delivered Him up for us all, how shall He not with Him also freely give us all things?" (Romans 8:32)

God did not go to all the sacrifice and effort of purchasing your soul, restoring you to Himself, and transforming your life just to leave you high and dry in the area of romance. Let Him be as big as He says He is, and you'll be able to say along with all those who have tasted of His faithfulness, "Now to Him who is able to do *exceedingly abundantly above all that we ask or think,* according to the power that works in us, to Him be glory in the church by Christ Jesus to all generations, forever and ever" (Ephesians 3:20–21, emphasis added).

> For I know the thoughts that I think toward you, says the
> LORD, thoughts of peace and not of evil, to give you a
> future and a hope.
>
> JEREMIAH 29:11

> Delight yourself also in the LORD, and He will give you the
> desires of your heart.
>
> PSALM 37:4

A Look Inside Your Heart

1. What do you hope for and desire in a spouse? Are your desires based on shallow, worldly standards, or are you seeking someone with the attributes of Christ?
2. What are the fears that compel some singles—even perhaps you—to search frantically for a spouse rather than waiting patiently on God?
3. Are you willing to wait for a Christlike girl or guy, or have you been lowering your standards out of impatience?
4. In what ways does God need to change your desires to match His desires for your life?

A Step Further

You've probably spent a good amount of time evaluating what you desire in a spouse. But have you ever stopped to gain God's perspective on the kind of person He desires to bring into your life? If you aren't sure, ask Him! Take some time to pray about it and seek His heart. Write down any thoughts, insights, or specific promises you feel He is speaking to you. Remember that the closer you draw to God, the more He will refine your desires to match His own. As you delight in Him, your desires will become His desires. Consider keeping a journal in which you write down all the desires you feel He has given you, and then record how He meets those desires in His own perfect time and way. God's ways may not look exactly the way you expect, but you will never be disappointed when the Author of romance holds the pen of your life. ✕

Eleven

Home Sweet Home

The ultimate test of true love

✕ ERIC ✕

When I was twelve, you were *pretty* cool if you could use the word "dude" five times in one sentence. You were *really* cool if your shoes stunk because you never wore socks. And you were *the epitome* of cool if you had a pair of corduroy OP shorts.

When I was twelve, shorts were really *short*. Corduroy OPs hugged your rear end like Saran Wrap around a grapefruit and seemed to hang maybe a fraction of an inch longer than a pair of Speedos. When these were in, they were really in. But when they went out of style, they *plummeted* out of style.

By the time I was thirteen, I had already donated my beloved tan OPs to Goodwill and was learning to do the moonwalk in parachute pants. (Yes, the eighties at their worst.) It was right at that time, at the height of my pubescent years, that my dad walked into a bargain basement and picked himself out a really cheap pair of totally outdated, fluorescent blue corduroy OPs.

"So, what do ya think?" he said to me, as he proudly modeled his "great discovery" in the middle of the living room while the blinds were open.

"Where did you get those?!" I howled in horror, leaping to close the blinds and spare the neighbors from witnessing this detestable fashion show.

"I got these babies for three bucks!" he proclaimed while doing a spin in front of the mirror and checking out his tightly packaged rear end.

"Dad legs" are a sight I believe every young person needs to behold at least once in a lifetime. If not for academic reasons, then just for a little peek into the way things are outside of Hollywood. But I'll warn you—wear your sunglasses! Dad legs see the light of the sun approximately once every ten years.

So there stood my dad in the middle of our living room. The light was off, but you would have never noticed because my dad's fluorescent blue shorts, accompanied by his glowing white "dad legs," were providing plenty of light.

Have you ever noticed that dads have no clue how to wear their socks either? At thirteen, I had started wearing socks again, but they were always scrunched down at the ankles. Dads, for some reason, never learn the cool way to wear socks. My dad was not only snuggled inside the most outdated and despicable pair of fluorescent blue shorts, with his "dad legs" glowing like the sun coming out of ten years' captivity, but he had his socks yanked up to his kneecaps. And just when you thought it couldn't get any worse…they were black dress socks!

A few weeks passed before I saw my dad in this deplorable ensemble again. But this time it wasn't in the safe confines of the Ludy living room. He unveiled it right smack in the middle of our family vacation, before the eyes of untold masses when the Ludy family went out to build a sandcastle on the beach.

"Well, wouldn't this make for a great picture!" my mom excitedly declared with her trusty camera in hand. "Okay now, let's all gather around." Then came the discovery. "Hey! Where's Eric?"

My dad was not only adorned in the OP shorts set off with black dress socks, but he had added a white V-necked undershirt to complete the look. I was a good three hundred yards away, pretending to shop for a metal detector. In fact, it would have taken a high-powered set of binoculars to see me. And if someone had come up to me and said, "Hey! Isn't that your dad over yonder?" I would have denied him three times before the cock crowed.

Disowning family members is not something we need to be taught how to do. It's something we just somehow become really good at. When my brother, Marky, was fifteen, he worked at Dairy Queen and wore polyester brown pants. He used to have my mom drop him off a quarter mile from work and tell her, "Okay! Now here's the plan. I'll call you when I'm done and I'll meet you right here. Make sure you don't come *there*!"

He would then proceed to hike to Dairy Queen and always make it look as if he was getting out of a really nice car in the parking lot. Then he would confidently stroll to the door of the restaurant, spinning a set of borrowed keys in his hand and whistling.

We are trained by our culture to be embarrassed about our family.

We are educated by our peers in the art of ignoring our parents' advice and belittling them with our words. In fact, in our teen years we are desperate to convince the world at large that we are lone rangers without a family, self-sufficient, and attending school purely for social reasons.

Many of us, over the years, have become professionals at living our lives without family. And most of us have very good reasons too. Reasons that go beyond our dad's glowing white legs. Reasons that touch us where we hurt and where we feel. If you want to touch a deep nerve in just about anyone, all you need to do is bring up the subject of family. Probably more than 90 percent of the pain and hurt in our lives stems directly from our homelife growing up.

For the vast majority of people, family doesn't seem to fit into the "beautiful side of love." In fact, it fits better into the "beautiful side of memory loss," when you are finally able to forget all that went wrong in your life.

Well, leaving out family when it comes to your love life is like baking bread without yeast—it will come out flat in the end. Now, it's important to understand that family means something different to each and every one of us. For some of us it means two parents, a brother, a sister, and a shaggy dog named Waldo. For others it means just a dad or maybe just a mom. There are some whose family consists solely of those few special people at church who care about them.

God designed us to be connected with family. Even if those who have a biological link to us are not near and familiar, He still provides special people in our lives who can fill in as Dad, Mom, big brother, little sister, and a shaggy dog named Waldo.

So no matter if you have a big family or a little family consisting of fill-ins from the little Baptist church down the street, this section, if taken to heart, will not only sweeten your love story, but it could very well change your life.

Them

There are four people on the Planet Earth who can irritate me quicker than any others. I have tremendous patience, boundless grace, and bottomless mercy for seemingly everyone except these four people.

I really do desire to be an example of Jesus to everyone I meet. I want people to walk away after spending time with me thinking, *That must be what Jesus acts like.* There are moments when I really think I'm getting there, but then...I get around one of "them."

Each of us has our "them." Maybe you don't have four; maybe you have two, or maybe you have twenty. But we all have "them." A good formula for finding the "them" in your life is to look for all of those who share your last name, always get a slice of your birthday cake, and have an exact replica of your nose stuck on their faces. "Them," in your life just as in mine, are familiar. Very familiar. You know everything about "them," from the bad jokes they always crack to their personal body fragrance.

Really, the only requirement for a "them" in our lives is *familiarity.* Or, if familiarity is too vague a word, how about this one: *family.* Everyone else in the world may be bamboozled into thinking that we are perfect angels, but our family knows the truth.

If you were to take a peek inside the windows of my home while I was growing up, you would have wonderful blackmail material on me now. I was a "Christian," but you wouldn't have ever confused me with St. Francis of Assisi. I was anything but Christlike as I roamed the hallways of my home.

In a matter of three seconds I could scream, "What are you doing? This is my room, you big stink. Get outta here!" "Hey! Turn it back! I was watching the game." "Meatloaf for dinner? I hate meatloaf!" For some reason most of us feel comfortable venting all of our pent-up frustrations on those who make the mistake of being related to us.

We demand that our families be perfect, and we don't allow room for error. Let me make a case in point. Growing up, if a random person accidentally stepped on my big toe—and I mean really squashed it—my response was quite a bit different than if my *brother* accidentally stepped on my big toe.

To the random person, I would offer grace and be polite. "I'm sorry!" they would apologize. And I would readily forgive them. "That's all right!" I'd respond, even if my face was fire-red with pain and my cheeks were bloated from containing my yelp. "These things happen. I'll survive!"

To most people on Planet Earth I would offer grace. Now my brother on the other hand…he should know better than to squash the big toe of his older brother. My response to him would have been a little more animated.

"Hey!" I would bellow in irritation. "What do you think you're doing? Watch where you're walking!" Then, as is appropriate for all good and healthy brotherly encounters, I would give him a hard shove.

It's difficult for us to extend grace to the "them" in our lives. We often expect "them" to live at a higher standard of perfection than anyone else on the planet.

But it doesn't stop here. Not only do those closest to us get under our skin and irritate us, but they also have the power to wound us in a way no one else can.

If you came up to me and said, "Eric, you stink, you're ugly, and I hate you!" I would probably step back, blink a couple of times, and then say, "Well, uh, thanks for being so blunt!" I would go home and tell Leslie about what you said and probably even feel rejected as I recalled the episode. Then Leslie would tenderly wrap her arm around my shoulders and say, "Eric, that's ridiculous! That person was probably on drugs or something."

Your words might sting for a little while and might cause me to dab on an extra puddle of cologne before I head out into public, but I *would* get over your words. Why? Because you're not my family.

If my *dad* came up to me and said, "Eric, you stink, you're ugly, and I hate you!" I would be absolutely devastated. Any number of comforting words from Leslie wouldn't be able to bandage up the wound my dad's words would inflict on my heart and mind. Your words would hurt, but my dad's words would cripple. Because *you* would just be giving an opinion, but *my dad* is my definition of reality.

Our generation is lying crippled on the side of life's road because of the words of those most familiar with us. You may think of yourself as stupid because those who knew you best when growing up always said you were. Or you may be convinced you are fat. Why? Because your family always told you that you were. Or you may view yourself as ugly simply because the word *ugly* has been used by your little brother to describe your face since you were in kindergarten. Family defines our reality. Even if they are lying or mistaken, we can't help but believe family—because if anyone should know, it's *them*!

No wonder so many of us abandon the family ship as soon as we get the chance. We want to escape the irritants, the bosses, the nitpickers, the know-it-alls.

But we just don't do well alone. We all desire to belong. God designed us for companionship and for teammates. So we head out into this great big world in search of a *different* family. Some of us try to find it in friends, some of us look for it in sports, and some of us even attempt to find it in our shaggy dog named Waldo. But when we run from "them" and try to meet our needs with our choice of fill-ins instead of God's choice, we will never cover the ache. We *need* family! We need our "them"! And believe it or not, family is not just the solution to loneliness but the secret ingredient to successful romance.

When we condition ourselves to run away and disown those who are most familiar with us, we're preparing ourselves for a disastrous future. Our lives consist of relationships. God designed us for family. Intimate family relationships are among the most difficult things we must deal with as humans, because closeness leads to the exposure of who we *really* are, inside and out. To help us prepare for the intimacy demanded in marriage, we have a very short period in life that God seems to give us for practice. The Denver Broncos have a pre-season in which they hone their football skills, study the plays, and scrimmage. In the same way, we all have our pre-marriage season in which we need to hone our family skills, study the relationship playbook, and learn how to be like Christ to the "them" in our lives so we can be like Christ to our future spouse.

Family isn't just in our past; it's very much in our future too. And I guarantee you that if you train yourself to model Christ *now* to those most familiar and close, you will be superb at it when you get married.

Our Practice Field

When I was nineteen, God took hold of my life. After I opened the door to the *clank, clank* of God's knock, all the excitement I previously had for the Denver Broncos went directly into my love relationship with Jesus Christ. Everywhere I went, I would tell people about Jesus, and everyone who knew me before "the change" thought I had just taken a dip in the loony pond. I was a new Eric! I was loving people, serving people, and even hugging people. I was a great big bundle of angelic compassion, except when it came time for me to go…home. Everywhere else, I was a changed man, throwing a great big love party! The problem was, my family never received the invitation.

I'll never forget the day a tall, lanky pastor of mine muttered the words that changed my perspective. I have heard many words in my life. Most of them have whizzed down my ear canal, never even slowing down for as much as an hors d'oeuvre before exiting out the other side. But these words stuck. "You are only as holy," he said, "as you are in your home."

I was a good Christian. I had given Jesus Christ my entire ship. I was learning to love, to guard the treasure of my purity, and to be faithful to my future spouse. I didn't know anyone else who was doing that. But God was showing me, *Eric, if you're not able to act like Jesus now with those most close and familiar, then what makes you think that when you get married you are going to be an example of Jesus to your wife? Eric, you are only as Christlike as you are Christlike around your family. If you start there, where it is most difficult to love, then it will be easy to display Christ everywhere else!*

When I was eight, my mom signed me up for piano lessons. I loved to tinker, but I hated the practice. Practice is the most grueling aspect of success. But when the day of the recital came, I was always very glad my mom had forced me to practice. Because I was prepared, I was a whole lot less likely to make a fool of myself in front of the crowd.

Family is our rehearsal for relationships. We take into our future marriage the skills we master with "them" in the here and now. If we learn to snub and disown those closest to us now, we're setting patterns for broken trust and emotional heartache in the future. If we make a practice now of verbally abusing our family members, we are conditioning ourselves to bite rather than bless in the future.

Learn to Forgive and Be Forgivable

Marriage is a lifestyle chock-full of asking forgiveness and offering forgiveness. There are days I ask Leslie over twenty-three times to forgive me. If offering mercy and forgiveness were an Olympic event, I believe she could easily win the gold.

Each of us should train for such an Olympic event. Learning to forgive takes hard work and many tears. It takes determination and a whole lot of help from God.

It might seem nearly impossible to forgive your family for some of the things they did while you were growing up. But if you make it your goal to forgive them as God has forgiven you, and if you actively pursue loving them the way Christ loves you, then you will not only have set your own heart free, but you will have showcased a little picture of heaven on earth. If you learn to forgive, you will have learned the greatest defense strategy against divorce.

As a proper thank-you to God for selecting you for this new life of love, put on the clothes that He purchased for you and so generously placed in your spiritual closet: compassion, kindness, humility, silent confidence, and patience. Not haughty, hurtful, and holding grudges; but humble, helpful, and happy to forgive those who have wronged you just as thoroughly as Jesus forgave you. But more important than any other piece of clothing in your entire wardrobe, put on love. It's the key to the entire outfit, bringing out the sparkle in all the other elements.

COLOSSIANS 3:12–14 (PARAPHRASE)

Forgiving is hard. But oftentimes, it is even more difficult to be *forgivable*. Most of us complain about how we have been wronged by our families, but we fail to realize that we ourselves have been guilty of hurting them too. Let me show you a little video clip from my life.

Marky

Growing up as an older brother, I had a sacred duty: to make sure my younger brother, Marky, realized he was nothing but a dirtball. Older brotherhood is an art. I learned how to be a tough older brother by watching Tim Miller, the gargantuan big brother of my good friends Danny and Darren.

Tim had a wounded-mule strut, and as he walked he would snarl and move his mouth around as if he were chewing on a huge wad of gum. When he came strolling through the living room one day, I remember blurting out with my high, squeaky twelve-year-old voice, "Hey, Tim!"

His response was legendary. He boomed, "Hey!" in the deepest, most bassy voice I had ever heard. Then he did a little head nod with his eyes all squinty and strutted out of the room.

From that day on, whenever I spoke to Marky, it was with my best rendition of a bassy voice blended perfectly with the head nod and the squinty eye.

Big brotherhood is easy for some. But not for me! I just had to get stuck with a little brother who was two and a half years younger but looked older than me. All of our years growing up, Marky was a half-inch shorter than me, but he weighed more. He, of course, was built like a linebacker. And as my mom told me, "Well, Eric, you're just built more like a golfer!"

Well, I didn't want to be a golfer. I wanted to be a football player! God had somehow messed up and given Marky the brawn He was supposed to have given me. Since I was certain my scrawniness was a direct result of Marky's presence in my life, I was determined to make him pay.

For twenty years I never once spoke a compliment to my little brother. In fact, as the years passed, I became more cruel and more heartless. Don't get me wrong, I loved him; I just would never allow him to know that. He was my emotional punching bag, my stress reliever. I stuffed my anger all day long and then vented it on him.

There was also a brotherly pride that served as steel armor around my heart. I could never lose at anything to him. I could never show any tender emotion in front of him. And *never* would you catch me giving him a hug of any kind.

At every Ludy Family Christmas, one of our biggest traditions is to get up and hug the person whose gift you've just opened. This presented a problem whenever I opened my brother's Christmas present to me. There was no possible way I was going to drape these cool big brother arms around my stinkin' little brother's body. He had no desire to hug me either, so we invented our own version of the Christmas thank-you. We called it "The Bump."

With an arrogantly detached voice I would mutter, "Thanks." Then Marky and I bumped elbows and strutted like wounded mules back to our respective seats.

All my growing-up years, I referenced the world's pattern rather than God's to figure out successful behavior in relationships. At the age of twenty, I was still strutting around, still droning with my bassy voice, and still criticizing those closest and dearest to me. Before I was ready for a family of my own, I had to learn to bring the example of Jesus into my own home.

Discovering a Best Friend

It was just a normal night in March. I had no idea it was a night of destiny. I was home from college, my grandparents were visiting, and I was booted out of my room and stuck in my brother's room, next to his bed on a cot. I probably came into Marky's hangout and threw my stuff on the cot and boomed with my tough, raspy voice, "I'm sleeping in here!"

I was the same old Eric when I entered his room that night, but when I left in the morning, I was a new man. I remember trying to get comfortable on the stonelike mattress and staring up at the light fixture on the ceiling. My night of destiny began to unfold midway through my nightly conversation with God.

"Jesus, make me like You!" I remember boldly stating. "Whatever it takes, make me like You!" It wasn't but a millisecond later that God responded. I often jokingly warn people to be careful about what they pray. Even if you don't take what you pray seriously, God sure does! In fact, if you want to know God exists, pray that prayer. He just loves to respond to it!

In that moment, with my eyes fixed upon the ceiling, I knew beyond a shadow of a doubt what God wanted me to do. I call it the blowfish feeling. I knew precisely what I needed to do, but I also knew there was no possible way I could ever do it. I felt like my body was expanding and I was going to blow up! My palms were moist, and my heart was banging around inside my rib cage like a toddler with a kitchen pot.

If you have younger siblings, you will totally relate. As an older brother, I had become a master at making my younger brother feel worthless. Now, after an entire lifetime of criticism and cruelty, how was I supposed to…ask his forgiveness? Ten thousand tender and tear-filled hugs with my brother sounded better than that!

"God, I can't!" I mournfully remonstrated. "I know I just prayed that prayer, but there is just no way I can do that!"

As I anxiously rustled on the rock-hard cot that fateful night, feeling like a blowfish about to explode, I had to make a choice—a choice between relational stupidity and relational success. But even more directly, it was a choice between my big ego and my little brother.

My deep voice, which was usually lower than a snake's belly, squeaked like a parakeet going through puberty as I said, "Marky?"

All my older brother toughness dropped to the ground with one gigantic thud, as my little brother responded with *his* tough bassy drone, "Yeah?"

"Marky?" I again haltingly sputtered. "Uh…I don't quite know how to say this, but…I…I'm sorry." Silence filled the room and tears filled my eyes. My brother hadn't seen tears in my eyes since the time I stuck a kitchen knife into an electrical outlet when I was four. Now here I was, swallowing hard, with my lip quivering, right in front of him!

"I've been a horrible brother," I confessed. "I have never once complimented you. I have only torn you down. I've spent my life telling you what you do wrong, but I've never told you about all that you do right. I have built up so much pride between us, Marky!"

With tears flowing down my cheeks, I said, "Please forgive me! I really want to be your friend and not just your brother."

With all the things I had done to Marky over the years, he could have very easily laughed and left the room. I wouldn't have blamed him. But I'll never forget Marky's wet eyes looking into mine. His words were full of sincerity and love. "I forgive you."

We prayed together as a twosome for the very first time. If ever in my life I have been convinced God was smiling, it was during that prayer. I'm certain all heaven was listening.

When we concluded our first prayer as true brothers, I knew there was one more thing God wanted me to do.

"God, you are really pushing it!" I groaned.

I looked over at Marky and whispered, "Uh, there's something else I think we, uh (gulp), need to do."

All Marky said was, "I know."

We both got up from our beds, opened our arms wide, and *hugged* for the very first time!

I have often said that I discovered my best friend that plain, ordinary March night. But what I also discovered was the beautiful truth of how to have a successful relationship with those closest and most familiar. You have to learn to be forgivable.

I would guess that, whether you're an only child or had to take a number to get into the bathroom each morning, you can identify with my Marky story in some way, shape, or form. We all have our "them." We all need to realize that God has given "them" to us for the sake of practice. If you learn to be forgiving and forgivable with those in your life now, you will be great at it with your future family as well.

A wise older man once told me, "Humility is measured by how quickly you can admit that you are wrong."

Well, by that definition, I was one proud guy when I was growing up. Maybe you can relate. But it's never too late to discover success in relating to those closest to us. If we make a conscious decision today to seek humility, God can turn all our past haughtiness into evidences of His wondrous grace in our lives.

Learn to Cherish "Them"

Yes, family can be embarrassing at times! My dad had his fluorescent blue shorts, and my mom sang the "Hallelujah Chorus" in the grocery store checkout line—one of her many creative and loud ways to be a Christian witness. My sister was voted "most quiet" by her classmates, and Marky was…well…Marky.

Do not pray for easy lives!
Pray to be stronger men.
Do not pray for tasks equal to your powers.
Pray for powers equal to your tasks.
Then the doing of your work shall be no miracle,
but you shall be a miracle.[1]

PHILLIPS BROOKS

Those closest to us often seem like oddballs. We tend to think that everyone else on the planet is normal, but our family is from outer space.

"My dad has hair growing out of his ears, and he thinks it makes him look distinguished!" griped one person who wrote to us. "My mom takes her gum out at dinnertime and sticks it behind her ear for later!" complained another individual who desires to remain nameless. The truth is, we all have idiosyncrasies. We all have our own version of hair-ridden ears with gum stuck behind them.

Learning to loyally stand by those who embarrass us is a character trait of Christ. Just think: where would you be with God right now if He didn't hang around those of us who embarrass Him? Loyalty is also a necessary quality in a successful marriage relationship. When you get married you'll understand that even your spouse has oddball characteristics.

Leslie's parents told me before I married her, "Eric, the little quirks that you and Leslie both have can either be a source of irritation in your relationship or a source of humor and enjoyment. You need to learn how to cherish the funny little things both of you do!"

I like that word *cherish*. If we learn how to find intimate pleasure in the unique way God has crafted those closest to us, we could turn what usually causes us to run away into an opportunity for great enjoyment and fun.

My family has learned to laugh at all of our oddball characteristics. When we get together, we just howl about my dad's OPs. We chuckle with fondness as we reminisce about my mom singing the "Hallelujah Chorus" in the checkout line. And tears come to our eyes because we're laughing so hard when we talk about all that poor Leslie has to put up with in being married to a Ludy. Just imagine what Leslie thought the first time she saw me having a serious business conversation on the phone at five in the morning with nothing on but my tighty-whities. To Leslie, that was outrageous; to me, that was business as usual.

We each have a choice. We can either brand our families as embarrassing, or we can learn to take delight in their craziness. We can either run from them, thinking we're saving our precious reputations, or we can learn to be like Christ and cherish their nerdy side right along with their nice, neat, and noble side. Because *that* is what marriage is all about. Just ask Leslie!

Then Peter came to Him and said, "Lord, how often shall my
brother sin against me, and I forgive him? Up to seven
times?" Jesus said to him, "I do not say to you, up to seven
times, but up to seventy times seven."

MATTHEW 18:21–22

And be kind to one another, tenderhearted, forgiving one
another, even as God in Christ forgave you.

EPHESIANS 4:32

A Look Inside Your Heart

1. How would your interactions with family members change
   if you viewed your family as a practice field for healthy
   relationships?
2. In reading this chapter, have you thought of any family
   members you have wronged? If so, what steps could you
   take to seek forgiveness and repair the relationship—even
   if they don't acknowledge their part in the offense?
3. What do you appreciate most about each of your family
   members? How can you cultivate a heart of appreciation
   instead of irritation toward them?

A Step Further

If you want to excel in your future family, a key step is becoming a
reflection of Christ in your current family. Forgiveness is one of the
most difficult things God asks of us. And yet it is also one of the most
important of His requests. Christ says that we receive forgiveness
according to the measure that we offer it (Matthew 6:12). Take some
time to read the powerful account of forgiveness and reconciliation in
Genesis 44 and 45. Ask God to prepare your heart to make things
right with your family members. Do you need to write someone a

letter? Make a phone call? Sit down and talk? Whatever He places on your heart to do, don't let another day go by before you obey. Even if it is simply forgiving them in your own heart rather than unnecessarily reopening wounds, don't delay for another moment. Leaning upon the enabling power of Christ in you, you can choose right now to let them off your hook and place them on God's hook. This means you no longer hold their wrongdoing over them; you have given their offense to God for Him to deal with as He sees fit. As Corrie ten Boom once observed, "Forgiveness is not an emotion [but] an act of the will." Once we make the choice to forgive, she said, God will "supply the feeling."[2]

Twelve

The Secret to Winning a Heart

The best training ground for romance

✕ ERIC ✕

'll never forget my mom, with her hands on her hips and a scowl on her face, pounding this point home to her disagreeable fourteen-year-old son. "Eric, the way you treat *me* is the way you are going to treat your *wife*!"

My response was anything but remorseful and sweet. I countered, "I'm gonna treat her better than that!"

I was convinced that when my wife came into my life, my knight-in-shining-armor side would finally appear and I would treat her like a princess. I mean, I loved my mom and all, but not like that! When my radiant lover came into my life, I would be mesmerized with her beauty. I was certain that married life would tap into my sweeter, more sensitive side. Unfortunately for both you and me, that is just not true.

Sure, it is true that your spouse will hold a place in your heart, mind, and life that your mom or dad could never fill. And it's true that it will be easier at first to put your most sensitive foot forward. But it is also true that the closer and more familiar you get with your spouse, the more your true self will seep out. And the person you have spent your life training to become will be unveiled. For most of us, that is not a good thing.

Leslie has thanked God a myriad of times for the season in my life when He taught me how to treat my mom and sister with sensitivity. For three years, from the age of twenty to the age of twenty-three, I made it one of my primary focuses in life to practice being a true gentleman. It wasn't easy! Not because of them but because of me. I had gotten so used to spouting off whatever thoughts came into my mind. I had to learn that women take words a little more seriously than men do. Statements such as, "Are you really going to wear that dress?" and "Boy, you look totally exhausted!" and "Whoever cooked this stroganoff needs to learn how to use an oven!" and "Are you pregnant or just preparing for winter?" were now completely off-limits.

It was during this three-year period that I learned to get up after dinner and, without even being asked, immediately wash the dishes. Now, guys, don't ask me why, but that dishwashing thing has a powerful effect on women! I also learned, though I was scared to death of the answer, to simply ask, "Is there any way I can help?"

> *What am I to do? I expect to pass through this world but once. Any good work, therefore, any kindness, or any service I can render to any soul of man…let me do it now. Let me not neglect or defer it, for I shall not pass this way again.*[1]
>
> AN OLD QUAKER SAYING

There are two ways each of us can approach life: spending our days meeting our needs or looking for ways to meet others' needs. The mystery is that when we spend our life focused on our own needs, we are never satisfied and our deepest needs never seem to be met. But when we pour out our life and focus on how we can serve others, not only do we find incredible fulfillment, but our deepest needs are met as well! Learning to serve leads to the "happily ever after" finish you've always dreamed of.

Appreciating the Differences

I'm convinced, after studying the female of the species for twenty-eight years, that girls wear perfume not to impress us guys but to impress other girls! Just think about it. If a girl really wanted to douse herself in a fragrance that would magnetically pull a guy to her side, she would pour on something that smelled like a spicy chicken burrito.

The same is true with us guys. We lift weights, grunt, sweat, pull hamstrings, twist ankles, and stink, all to impress the girls when, in actuality, it's mostly other guys who take notice of such things. When we guys see a chiseled and musclebound hulk, we think with admiration, *Wow! He's huge!* Most girls only get disgusted by the fact that he's wearing spandex.

Another thing I've learned through careful observation is that if you want to win a heart, you need to be tender. Tenderness is the quality of slipping into someone else's world and caring for them in the way their world defines as "the best way of meeting my needs."

Part of what makes marriage both fun and exciting is learning to appreciate the little things your spouse works so hard at. Leslie has very little appreciation for an enormous muscle. Which is really a good thing, because if she did, she wouldn't have married me. My build is what my mom calls wiry. I have absolutely no excess *anything* on my body. I don't have a spare tire around the middle, but I don't have a whole lot of spare muscle hanging out on my body either. If I stop lifting weights for just one week, I shrivel up like a raisin on a hunger strike, and I'm at risk of the next big gust of wind carrying me away. So I work hard at keeping weight on, especially muscle. And Leslie, the student of Eric Ludy that she is, has learned how important it is that she notice my muscles, even if they are miniuscule.

Girls, it might not make any sense to you, but when you act impressed over something that a man works hard at, even something as small as one of my muscles, it makes him feel like a champion.

The same thing happens in reverse when I crawl into Leslie's world and learn to appreciate the little things that she works hard at. Leslie is a great shopper. I am not. I am very good at saving money, not spending it. Leslie is very good at what she calls "saving money while spending it." A very subtle difference, but one that has ruined more than a few marriages. As weird as this might sound, I have learned to have fun shopping with Leslie. I have made it a point to spend time in her world and attempt to enjoy myself. Leslie would note that my grumbling and grumpy side can still surface during such shopping ventures, but all in all we have learned to have a great time together searching for just the right sweater for those pants and the appropriate belt to go with that shirt.

When two people get married they inevitably discover that each of them is very different from the one to whom they just said, "I do." We cover up a lot of those differences when we are falling in love, but marriage is total nakedness. Who we are behind all our fine apparel is seen in all its glory when we move in together. Leslie used to think my breath always smelled like wintergreen Binaca. When she woke up next to me one newly wedded morning and caught a whiff of the "breath of death," she found out how wrong she was!

Shut Up and Snuggle

Leslie and I had been married for about three weeks when she began to act sort of funny. There she was, sitting on the end of our bed, crying. The problem was, she was crying for no reason. As a guy, I cry when I have something to cry about—which is almost never. But Leslie, I discovered, sometimes cries just to cry.

I sat down next to her and said, "Les? What's wrong?" You see, as a guy, I like to figure out the problem. Why? So I can fix it! "Come on, Les! Tell me what happened so I can help!"

What really confused me was that Leslie cried even harder after I offered help. You would think she would want me to help fix her life. I mean, if I were crying, that's what I would want her to do for me. Right there was my problem. As long as I tried to meet Leslie's needs in the way I desired my needs to be met in my world, I only made things worse. The only way I can help Leslie is when I crawl into her world and look at meeting her needs through her eyes. What I find is shocking.

She wants me to shut up! Strangely, she doesn't even want her problem solved. She just wants me to be there, to validate her feelings, and to wrap my arm around her shoulder and squeeze—to show that I care, that I empathize, and that I take her feelings seriously.

Women seem to think it is obvious that a guy should just know to do that. But it's the furthest thing from our minds. Since we, as guys, usually want our problems solved, we naturally feel that the best way to be sensitive to a girl would be to help her solve her problems too. Despite the fact that we guys are often bumbling idiots when it comes to sensitivity, we really are trying!

Guys, being a shoulder to cry on, speaking words that remind a woman of your affection, doing the dishes after dinner, and making sure she has a full tank of gas before she hits the road to go shopping—these are all simple little things that you can do to tenderly care for a woman. Because in her world, these little things are huge.

Girls, if you want a few hints on winning a guy's heart, just talk with Leslie. She is the absolute best at it! You know what she calls me? Her hero. She knows that the way to grab a guy's heart is to ennoble him with words. When a man is respected and honored by a woman, he gains thirty-six pounds of sheer muscle instantly, can outrun a bullet train, and can leap a skyscraper in a single bound. Words of respect transform mere men into superheroes. So whether it is squeezing his muscles, showing interest in his rock collection, or calling him your hero, a dash of tenderness in the way you treat a man means the difference between being married to a gentle-man or a gingerbread-man. One is heroic and tender; the other is stale and cut out of the same mold as the rest of them.

> *Be careful not to allow any words that are dirty, disrespectful, or damaging slip from your lips. Use your words to build, not burden; to help, not harm; and to encourage, not exasperate.*
>
> EPHESIANS 4:29 (PARAPHRASE)

If you are going to successfully win the heart of your lover someday, you need to start practicing tenderness now. And just like learning to forgive and be forgivable, and learning to cherish and to serve, your practice ground is none other than your family.

I guarantee you that if you can learn to be sweet and tender with the "them" in your life, your future lover's heart will be putty in your hands.

Moms and Sisters

Guys, if your mothers and sisters are still in near proximity to where you are living, they are wonderful training wheels for learning how to navigate the confusing world of women. I recommend mothers and sisters not only because they are the most difficult to practice on, but also because they are some of the few women on the planet who won't misinterpret your tenderness as a proposal for marriage. If you don't have a mother or sister, just use extreme discretion on whom you choose to practice. Because tenderness really does work!

Okay now, guys, if tenderness is a foreign concept to you, then putting it into practice will be a bit strange at first. But I promise, the more you do it, the more natural it will seem. First, look for opportunities to compliment these dear women in your life. Whether it is their hair, their stunning outfit for church, their amazing singing voice, or even their incredible sense of humor, learn to notice the little things that are important in their world.

Second, voice your admiration out loud. Tell them how beautiful they look, how nice their voice sounds, or how fun they are to be around. They will undoubtedly be shocked when you first transform into a gentleman, but your consistency will convince them that your self-focused, it's-all-about-me attitude is a thing of the past.

Third, learn to be a student of women. You might think that you already are, but most guys don't realize there is far more to a woman than just her physical beauty. You need to become a student of how a woman works on the inside. If you desire a "happily ever after" romance, you need to study the inner workings of the female gender.

I remember being nineteen and extremely *un*tender. My mom was having a bad hair day. Plus, she was teary and frustrated with the color of the kitchen cabinets; she thought the T-shirt I was wearing should be thrown out; and she thought my dad should tell his boss to jump in a frozen lake. Finally, at about three in the afternoon, she yelled out, "I just need to get out of this house!"

I was in the kitchen, approximately four feet from my mother, clothed in my raggedy T-shirt. I carefully considered the words my mom had just spoken and then flippantly replied, "You just went to the store today."

Let my experience serve as a warning to all men. Never respond to a woman the way I did in that scene. When a woman speaks, there is a difference between the precise definition of what she says and the actual meaning behind her words. When a woman says, "I just need to get out of this house," her meaning goes far beyond walking out onto the front porch and watching neighborhood traffic pass by. I still don't have it figured out, but I think it has more to do with a candlelit dinner out, purchasing a new outfit from Saks Fifth Avenue, and a quick stop by the jewelry store just to browse and drop hints. But only a student of women would pick up on that slight differentiation.

Finally, learn to just shut up and be a shoulder to cry on. And don't solve, just snuggle. When your mom or sister doesn't make sense, don't force her to be rational; rather, learn to place your arm around her shoulder and squeeze.

Dads and Brothers

Girls, I must admit that your training wheels for learning tenderness are a whole lot more challenging to put on. It is usually fairly easy for daughters to be tender to dads; it's brothers who pose the bigger problem.

Brothers like me tend to be 95 percent jerk, 4 percent gross, and 1 percent tender. Most sisters would probably say 1 percent is a little too generous! Basically, we are in desperate need of a little schooling when it comes to learning how treat a lady, let alone how to win her heart.

Sisters, this is where you come in. Please have mercy on us guys and learn to be tender with us. In fact, if only for the sake of the women we will one day marry, help prepare us to be true gentlemen. Look at it as a wedding gift to your future sister-in-law. Whether you realize it or not, a man is shaped by the words of a woman. Through words that belittle, even the strongest man in the world can be made a wimp. But through words that build up, even the biggest wimp can be transformed into a world leader.

First, crawl into a guy's world (wear a nose plug) and observe what in our world is important. Every guy is different, so you can't just say food and football. It might be music, computers, art, or any number of odd things you wouldn't expect.

Next, find opportunities to discuss these fascinating topics with him. If you venture into his world, you will discover that he really does have more to him than grunting and sweating. And just as you desire to hear words that make you feel cherished, we guys need to hear words that make us feel respected.

The next time you see your brother doing something he excels in, honor him with admiration of his prowess and let him know that you are proud to be his sister. You will find that the more you verbally invest respect, the more a man will understand how to be respectful himself.

And finally, don't try to change a guy to be more like a girl. Learn to appreciate manhood for all that God created it to be. Maybe it's not naturally as sweet and beautiful as womanhood, but with a little help from the women in our life, we can have a version of sweetness and beauty that is a perfect blend of toughness and tenderness and is 100 percent masculinity.

This might sound like a betrayal of the male species, but there are times when even we guys don't make sense. In those times, we too need a shoulder to cry on. So be ready with a listening ear, and never make a guy feel like an idiot for sharing his fears and deeper feelings.

A Sweetened Love Story

Let's get back to the sweeter song. We all long for the beautiful side of love and the happily ever after kind of romance. But are we willing to do what it takes to get it? As we discussed earlier in the book, the sweeter song is played in the life that empties itself for God, abandons itself to trust Him, and seeks to emulate Jesus with every action, attitude, and word. The sweeter song is more a gift than a goal. It's not something we earn; it is something we receive as we allow the Great Author of romance to masterfully shape us into gentle and sensitive lovers, just like our Bridegroom, Jesus.

Family, as I mentioned earlier, is a piece of our lives that many of us would rather discard. But the sweeter song is dependent upon your learning to forgive and be forgivable, to cherish those close and familiar, to serve those who often seem the most difficult to serve, and to tenderly care for the near and dear ones.

If you discard those oddballs in your life called family, you will have thrown away your own private training ground for a divine romance. If you don't learn now to be like Christ in the way you treat "them" in your life, it will be that much more difficult to treat your "them-of-the-future" with the dignity and love they will desperately need.

> Through love serve one another. For all the law is fulfilled
> in one word, even in this: "You shall love your neighbor as
> yourself."
>
> GALATIANS 5:13–14

> Be subject to one another in the fear of Christ.
>
> EPHESIANS 5:21 (NASB)

> Let nothing be done through selfish ambition or conceit, but
> in lowliness of mind let each esteem others better than himself.
> Let each of you look out not only for his own interests, but
> also for the interests of others.
>
> PHILIPPIANS 2:3–4

A Look Inside Your Heart

1. Are you treating your current family the way Jesus would treat them? In what practical ways can you become more of a reflection of Christ and show tenderness in these relationships?

2. If the key to winning someone's heart is to crawl into that person's world, how could you go about doing that?

3. In what circumstances do you find it most difficult to serve family members or demonstrate tenderness? How could facing up to this challenge help prepare you for a healthy relationship with your future spouse?

A Step Further

In a culture that advocates looking out for number one, putting others first takes deliberate effort and practice. Spend some time today thinking about each family member and how their world and needs compares with your own experience. Prayerfully consider the ways your words and actions may have caused hurt or misunderstanding. Then, as you think about each person, invite God to give you some creative ideas for how to serve your parents and siblings in a meaningful way. Ask Him to show you how to love your neighbor without leaving home. ✄

Thirteen

Playing for Keeps

How to pick a winning team

✖ LESLIE ✖

As a sixteen-year-old new driver, I was a serious safety hazard to the state of Colorado. Yes, I had taken driver's ed classes, but I had spent most of those hours writing notes to friends or dozing off, rather than actually learning anything about the important skills needed to operate a motor vehicle.

When I finally got my license (don't ask me how I passed the driver's test) I was so excited to have my freedom. I supposedly no longer needed my parents to accompany me whenever I took the car out on the open road. I was absolutely convinced I could do it alone.

There were a few minor details I had failed to learn while snoozing in driver's ed class. However, I was confident that I would easily figure out anything I might have missed once I actually got out there and started driving.

One bright January afternoon, I needed to drive across town for an appointment. My parents nervously eyed me as I grabbed the car keys and headed out the door. "Do you want someone to go with you, Leslie?" they questioned.

"I don't need help," I informed them with an offended look, as if they had just offered to cut my pancakes into bite-size pieces for me. They glanced at each other in genuine concern but decided to let me go alone anyway. I excitedly bounced out to the car, jumped in, cranked up the radio, and stepped on the gas.

As I pulled up to an intersection and coasted into the left turn lane, all reason abandoned me. Was I supposed to go *around* the median? Or turn in front of it? There were no cars coming the other direction to help me see which way to turn, and I began to panic. As the arrow turned green, I brilliantly concluded that I should turn in *front* of the median rather than going around it. At that moment a car came toward me, head-on, and I realized I had just made a not-so-subtle driving mistake! My mind raced. *I don't think they covered this in driver's ed,* I concluded, as I pondered what to do next. The oncoming traffic that was rapidly collecting angrily honked at me. I shakily backed out of the wrong lane and went *around* the median, my cheeks burning with humiliation. It was one of my more embarrassing moments, and I could only hope that none of the other drivers recognized me.

One of the traits we naturally possess as humans is the headstrong determination to do things *our* way, and to do things *alone.* In our culture it is seen as a sign of weakness to seek help from someone else. And yet, as Christians, God designed us to need one another. He designed us to lean upon the body of Christ for support, prayer, wisdom, and even practical help. Stubbornly taking the wheel and driving off all alone, without assistance from others, will lead us straight into oncoming traffic and sometimes even cause a head-on collision. This is especially true in our love lives.

Choosing a Team

One of the most common questions of a single person who longs for a God-written love story is, "How will I know when a relationship is from God?"

To help answer that perplexing question, and to prepare for real success in romance, one of the best things you can do is develop a team. Your team should be made up of godly people who can keep you accountable to your commitments, pray with you, and provide a refreshing outside perspective on the ups and downs of your journey through life.

Look at the people in your life whom God may have provided for that very purpose. When you find your teammates and invite them to share in this part of your life, you will discover a sense of beauty and security you never knew was possible.

No longer will you have to figure things out on your own; you will be supported by people who love you and will stand beside you. These teammates can provide confirmation and wisdom in helping you discern God's will for your love life.

Why Parents Make Good Teammates

For most of us, the most obvious teammates God has given to us are our parents. I know, I know…that notion may not sound very appealing. Parents often seem to be the antithesis of romance. However, I am not talking about prearranged marriages. And I am not talking about surrendering your love life to your parents. I am simply suggesting that you invite your parents to be on your team as you seek God's heart for your love life. You might be surprised by what happens when you do. Here's why parents make such great teammates:

1. *Parents have an intrinsic, God-given wisdom for their child's life.* When we are young it usually drives us crazy, but as we mature, this wisdom is something we learn to cherish. It can be invaluable when we are confused over a relationship. Whether or not we appreciate their advice, the opinions of our parents should definitely be evaluated seriously before God.

2. *When we honor our parents' God-given position in our life, we honor God.* He will bless our decision to honor our parents, even if it isn't easy (see Ephesians 6:1–3).

When I began to learn how to give God the pen to write my love story, one of the first things I felt Him lead me to do was to invite my parents to be on my team through prayer and accountability. It was as if He told me, *Leslie, I have placed your parents in your life for a reason. I have given them a wisdom and anointing, especially for your life. Don't ignore the built-in teammates I've provided for you.*

Yet I was uncomfortable with the thought of my parents being involved in my love life. After all, I had grown up in a culture that taught me to become independent of my parents. I was a young adult, living responsibly. Why did I suddenly need my parents' help? Though I was making my own decisions and my parents were treating me as an adult, I still somehow pictured them seeing me as a twelve-year-old in need of strict supervision when it came to this area of my life.

I imagined hesitantly telling them, "Okay, Mom and Dad, I really want your help in discerning God's will for my love life."

Then I pictured them rubbing their hands together with wicked glee and replying, "Well, it's about time! We have already decided that you shouldn't get married for ten more years, and we'll pick out your husband for you."

That scenario couldn't have been further from reality. My parents were just as concerned with my happiness as I was. And when I came to them and invited them to be "on my team" and help me seek a godly love life, they responded quite differently than in my wild imaginings.

"Leslie, we love you. You and your brothers are more important to us than anything else in the world. We have been praying for your future husband since the day we became Christians. We don't have things all figured out, but we want you to know that we are here for you any time you need us. We will pray with you whenever you need it, and we will try to provide you with support during these important years of your life."

The freedom and security that came with their words was amazing! The first step had been giving God the pen to write my love story—learning to trust Him completely. He had set the stage perfectly by forming a beautiful team relationship between my parents and me. I didn't have to walk this path alone! I had two people who dearly loved me and wanted the best for me, and who were committed to seeking God with me and supporting me every step of the way.

It was incredible how God wrote each line of my love story with Eric just at the perfect time. Little did I know how important that conversation with my parents would be to the rest of the script.

3. *Honoring your parents can actually make your love story more beautiful.* Believe me, I never would have thought that adding parents to the picture could possibly bring romance. But some of the most unforgettably romantic moments in my love story with Eric involved our parents.

Eric and I had a close friendship for many months before anything romantic happened between us. In fact, neither one of us would have ever expected a deeper relationship to develop because we were five years apart in age and I saw him as a godly older brother. But there came a point when we both began to ponder some questions about our friendship. Even if we were just friends, was it possible we were spending too much time together? Individually, we both had promised God that even our friendships with the opposite sex would be completely pure and honoring to our future marriage partner. Now we wondered, if our future spouses came into our lives, would they be comfortable with how much time we were spending together?

One summer day, while we were riding in a van together on the way home from a short-term mission outreach to inner-city New Orleans, Eric brought up the subject. "I want to honor and respect my future wife, and your future husband," he said. "My friendship with you is so important to me, but sometimes I wonder if we are *too* close. Maybe we are spending too much time together. It might be good for us to spend some time apart, praying about this."

As I nodded my head in agreement, Eric made another unexpected statement. "And maybe I should get together with your dad."

Without thinking, I replied, "Yeah, I think you should."

A moment of strained silence followed as we pondered our verbal missteps. Each of us was wondering why in the world we had agreed that Eric should talk to my dad. It wasn't as if he was going to ask for my hand in marriage or anything. We both were too embarrassed to bring it up again, however.

We soon found out that God knew exactly what He was doing in guiding our conversation along those lines. A few days later, Eric met my dad for lunch at a nearby restaurant. Eric nervously sipped his water as my dad studied the menu.

Why am I doing this? What am I even going to say? Eric wondered for the hundredth time. However, since he was already there, he determined to make the best of it. Once they had ordered, Eric took a deep breath and began his prepared speech.

"Rich, um, I just wanted to talk to you about my friendship with Leslie," he started, as my dad calmly gazed across the table at him. Eric swallowed awkwardly, then continued.

"I mean, I just want to be careful. Leslie and I are spending a lot of time together, and I want to honor her future husband and my future wife in this whole thing. I'm just wondering if you have any suggestions for how much time we should be spending together."

My dad was silent a moment or two. Then he began to share a few words of wisdom that Eric would never forget. "Eric, one of the reasons I know your friendship with Leslie is from God," he said confidently, "is because ever since you have been in her life, I've seen her only draw closer to God as a result of the friendship."

One of the beautiful things about having teammates is that they provide an outside perspective on a friendship or a relationship. They can see things that we are sometimes blinded to. Our teammates can help us determine whether or not a relationship is from God based on the fruit they see in our lives as a result of the relationship. If the relationship is drawing us away from God and other priorities, we need to seriously reevaluate things. However, if the friendship or relationship is drawing us closer to God and producing godly fruit in our lives, that could be evidence that God Himself has brought us together.

Our teammates can see our life from the outside, and therefore help us discern what is really going on. My parents had observed the positive effects of my friendship with Eric. They were able to clearly see that Eric inspired and encouraged me to have even a deeper love and passion for the Lord.

With my dad's insightful words, Eric realized all the more the value of having strong godly mentors, such as our parents, to come to with questions like the ones burning on his heart. My dad wasn't finished imparting timeless wisdom, however. His next phrase startled Eric but taught him an incredible truth.

"Eric," my dad continued, "I know your relationship with my daughter is pure. If your relationship with Leslie wasn't pure, God would tell me."

At such a bold statement, Eric's heart nearly stopped. *God* would tell him? At that moment Eric was weak with relief that our friendship had indeed been pure. He could just imagine how terrible it would be to have God wake my dad up in the night to tell him that it wasn't pure. Eric envisioned my irate father chasing him down the street with a shotgun.

That comment helped Eric realize a profound truth. He had always thought of me as an individual, independent and making all my own decisions. Now he realized God had put a protective covering over my life—the authority of my parents. God had given me to my parents as a treasure they were to care for, provide for, and protect. In that flash of realization, he saw how wrong it would be for him to ever pursue a romantic relationship with me without first honoring the position God had given my parents.

From that moment on, Eric decided that his parents as well as mine were going to be involved in our relationship from the beginning. He made a commitment to honor and respect the position of both his parents and mine.

Before he could ponder these new thoughts any longer, my dad made one final comment. "Eric, I just want you to know that Janet and I give you our blessing to pursue a relationship with our daughter in any way God would lead you."

Eric stared at him a moment. Had Rich misunderstood his intentions? He tried to clarify. "Rich, actually, that's not what I'm after at all…"

My dad held up his hand to interrupt. "I know," he said, "but for some reason, I just felt like I should give you that freedom."

Romance and Respect

Through an extraordinary series of events, it was only a few weeks later that Eric became sure that I was the one he would marry someday.

Eric was true to his commitment to honor and respect my parents' position in my life. He decided, after much prayer, to discuss this with my dad before talking to me about it. He had a pretty good idea of my feelings toward him, but he knew my dad would know better than anyone where I stood.

He again found himself sitting across the table from my dad at the same restaurant, this time early in the morning before work. But this time, he knew what he had come to say. As my dad sipped his coffee and tried to wake up, Eric dove right into the purpose of the meeting.

"Rich, after praying a lot about my friendship with Leslie over the past few weeks, I feel God has shown me that one day Leslie is going to be my wife."

Needless to say, my dad woke up pretty quick. But after a brief pause, he gave an amazing response.

"Eric," he said, looking him straight in the eye, "Janet and I have been praying for Leslie's future husband since the day we became Christians fourteen years ago. We prayed that we would recognize him when he came into her life. And, Eric, we've known for some time that you are the one."

What incredible confirmation! Eric was full of gratitude that God had allowed him to stumble onto the idea of getting together with my dad to discuss his friendship with me. He'd so often felt he was blundering his way through life, especially when it came to relationships. It was so reassuring to now have a strong teammate and wise counselor in the most unexpected person—his future father-in-law!

Eric's respect for my parents only deepened my appreciation for him. By the time this conversation took place, my heart was telling me that someday I would marry him. When I learned about their discussion, I realized all the more what a true man of integrity he was.

A few days later, my dad gave Eric the ultimate compliment. "I give you my blessing to win my daughter's heart."

When my dad gave Eric the blessing to "win my heart," he didn't just leave it there. After the relationship began, Eric and my dad met together on a regular basis...and my dad taught him *how* to win my heart. My dad knew me better than any other man in the world. And now he was passing his knowledge about me along to the man I would spend the rest of my life with. What girl wouldn't feel like a princess in that kind of scenario? The two most important men in my life were spending hours doing nothing but discussing who I was, how I was made, how Eric could understand me better, and how he could love me with the love of Christ.

I saw Eric's unwavering commitment to me. Eric was learning how to be sensitive to me, and with his determination to honor and respect my parents, my confidence in him grew strong and unshakable. I knew without a doubt he was the kind of man I wanted to be with for the rest of my life.

My parents were wonderful teammates. The months and years that followed built a bond between us that I never knew was possible. They showed their love to me in amazing ways: late-night talks and prayer sessions, little notes of encouragement, and doing everything they could to help make my relationship with Eric special. They even helped Eric coordinate the details of the night he proposed to me.

Inviting our parents to be our teammates as God scripted our love story was one of the best decisions we've ever made. Not only did it add excitement and romance to our relationship in ways we never could have dreamed, it also provided the strength and outside perspective we needed to make our love story successful. While Eric and I had the leading roles, the Great Author of romance had cast the perfect supporting characters. We couldn't have played our parts nearly as well without them.

When Parents Aren't in the Picture

When Eric and I share about our parents being involved in our love story, we often hear the comment, "Yeah, but who has parents like that? I think that part of your love story is a little too good for regular people who have messed-up families."

It is tragic that so many people are not blessed with loving and God-fearing parents. In a world where divorce, abuse, and abandonment run rampant, I must admit healthy families are becoming the exception rather than the rule. If your family is not what it should be, if your parents are not walking with the Lord, or maybe not even alive anymore, it's still important to have godly teammates. And there *is* hope, even when your parents aren't able or willing to join your team.

The beauty of God's ways cannot be limited by mere circumstance. He promises to be a "father of the fatherless" (Psalm 68:5). His loving heart goes out with compassion to those who don't have parents who can love and guide them. The beauty of the body of Christ is that, no matter the circumstances of our biological family, we have a spiritual family all around us. God can provide special people in your life to fill the position that your parents can't.

Just take a closer look at the ones who give you the most support—your pastor, your grandmother, or a godly mentor. Those people love you. Why not invite them to help you seek God in your love life? Most likely they will be honored and take their position as your teammate quite seriously.

Even if you are separated from your parents only by geography, it's important to have teammates nearby with whom you can walk through the journey of your relationship on a day-to-day basis. God is faithful to provide this type of support as well.

Amanda, a twenty-six-year-old exchange student from Canada, was studying in England, miles away from her parents, when she found herself drawn to a young man who came into her life.

"My parents were supportive in prayer for me, but I still needed someone to help me walk through the day-to-day stuff. Someone to whom I could make myself accountable and who could observe my relationship with this man on a regular basis," she told me. "I finally asked God to provide a father figure and a mother figure for me who could help me through the process of discerning God's will in this relationship."

God led her to her pastor and his wife, a couple who had learned to love Amanda like a daughter. They eagerly joined her in prayer about the young man in her life. When they felt they had wisdom to share with her, they did. They walked with her each step of the way as the relationship moved toward marriage.

"It was perfect," Amanda recalls. "God provided exactly what I needed through this couple. And the best part was that my pastor actually performed the wedding ceremony! God is so faithful!"

No matter what kind of relationship you have with your parents, God loves you like a faithful Father. He wants the best for you, and He will never let you down.

Playing to Win

Even though we live in a do-it-yourself world, it is dangerous to take that attitude toward relationships. The decision of who to spend the rest of your life with brings repercussions that will last for as long as you live. It's not a choice you should take lightly. And it's not a decision you should make alone.

Even if you are seeking God, it's wise to invite other perspectives into the picture. Not because God isn't capable of leading and guiding, but because we aren't always capable of listening and making the wisest choices on our own. As the writer of Proverbs eloquently reminds us:

> Without counsel plans fail, but with many advisers they
> succeed. (Proverbs 15:22, ESV)

But be warned: choose your teammates wisely. Just as godly input can help make a relationship successful, the wrong kind of counselors can lead to disaster. It might be tempting to invite your college roommate or your best friend to be your teammate and godly counselor in a relationship. But it's usually better to find someone older and wiser, someone with a bit more life experience and maturity, and—most important—someone who isn't going to just tell you what you want to hear.

Godly teammates not only can provide confirmation when God is putting a relationship together, but also can advise caution when something doesn't seem quite right. It's like having rearview and side-view mirrors while driving; they help us see things from a broader perspective. Their wisdom, experience, and maturity give them the ability to see the things we often miss. So don't just go the easy route when it comes to picking teammates. Be willing to submit to godly counsel from someone older, even if it seems difficult at first.

Jeff, a nineteen-year-old computer whiz, noticed a beautiful young woman at his church who had a genuine heart for God. As he built a friendship with her, he began to feel strongly that she might be the one he was to marry.

He prayed for a while about pursuing a relationship with her, but he was too stubborn to ask anyone else for advice on the subject, especially his parents. Though they were full of wisdom and loved him, he was out to prove that he could hear God on his own. He did ask a couple of his rather shallow "Christian" friends for their opinions. "Go for it, man," they all said confidently, without much thought. So Jeff dove headfirst into the relationship, but it soon exploded in his face. He hadn't taken time to have anyone pray with him or give him an outside perspective. He pursued things far too quickly and made a mess of the whole thing. Jeff deeply regrets his approach.

"It could have turned out great if I had just listened to the people in my life who really have wisdom," he admitted. "But I was so intent on doing things my own way that I ruined it. The few people I did ask for advice weren't really even qualified to give it."

Those people in your life who dearly love you and care about you, who are older, wiser, and have a lifetime of godly fruit to back up their words, are the best teammates you can pick. Who are the supporting characters God may be casting in your love story?

You don't need to wait until a relationship comes into your life to invite them to be on your team. From the time I was about twelve years old, a Christian couple who had been friends of our family for years began to faithfully pray for my future husband. Besides having my parents to turn to if I needed support, I also went to these friends from time to time to ask for prayer about specific situations. Thanks to God's provision, my teammates—my loving parents and other godly mentors—were in place long before my love story began.

When it comes to your love life, we're talking about one of the most important decisions you'll ever make—so choose your team carefully and play to win.

Where there is no counsel, the people fall; but in the multitude of counselors there is safety.

PROVERBS 11:14

"Honor your father and mother," which is the first commandment with promise: "that it may be well with you and you may live long on the earth."

EPHESIANS 6:2–3

A Look Inside Your Heart

1. What are the dangers of making relationship decisions without the benefit of outside perspective?

2. Are you willing to invite teammates to provide wise and godly counsel regarding your love life? If not, what concerns are holding you back? What, if anything, do you need to invite God to change about your attitude toward having godly counselors?

3. Are you open to having your parents be your teammates? Why or why not?

4. If your parents are unable to fill this role, who else in your life could serve in their place?

A Step Further

Prayerfully consider the people God has placed in your life to function as your teammates. (And remember not to disregard your parents for this role!) Plan a time to sit down and invite them to be on your team. Explain that you would like them to be your prayer support and to offer godly counsel and perspective as you navigate this area of your life. Even if you are not yet in a relationship, it's still a great idea to have your teammates in place long before one ever begins. Meet with your teammates on a regular basis for times of prayer and discussion. Allow them to be a voice of caution or confirmation as you consider whether or not to move forward in a relationship. Your teammates' opinion shouldn't replace the Spirit of God in your life, but rather be a beautiful enhancement to God's gentle leading and guiding. It may feel awkward to meet together and pray about this area, but the more you do it, the more you will realize what blessing and security it brings. ✕

Part Four

Happily Ever After

*Finding a Real-Life Fairy Tale
in the Midst of Modern Reality*

Fourteen

Too Late?

A glimmer of hope in a world of lost virginity

✕ LESLIE ✕

Her name was Rebecca, and she was only twelve. I met her at a church where Eric and I were speaking, and she told me her heartbreaking story.

Rebecca was a beautiful girl who looked much older than she was. Outwardly she seemed like a young woman, but inwardly she was still just a child. At church and at school, guys began to notice her—guys who were entirely consumed with fulfilling their own selfish, sexual whims. Rebecca mistook the attention of these young men for love and acceptance—things she had failed to receive from her parents growing up.

She met Jason at youth group. He was a good-looking, confident sixteen-year-old. Whenever he smiled at her from across the room, she felt something leap inside of her. Soon he was sitting with her every week, treating her as if he were a protective and caring older brother.

Her child's heart embraced the sense of security and warmth he brought to her, while the woman she was becoming began to feel a new and exciting attraction to him. As the weeks passed, her infatuation grew, as did her complete trust in this charming young man.

One night Jason invited Rebecca over to his house while his parents were out of town. Rebecca entered Jason's home as an innocent child of twelve, but hours later she left as a used and defiled sex toy. Overnight, Rebecca was forced from childhood into womanhood—but in the most unnatural and heart-wrenching way imaginable. She had lost her virginity before she had even fully developed physically or emotionally.

Rebecca was devastated and confused. Jason was finished with her and on to new prey.

Todd was an outgoing premed student at a Christian college in California. He had a deep love for the Lord and a passion to serve others. In spite of his heavy class load, Todd was actively involved in several campus ministries. He also led worship once a week at his local church. His long-term dream was to become a medical missionary.

He met Karly at an early morning prayer meeting he was leading. She was attractive, funny, and intelligent. Todd was fascinated by her. They met for coffee and ended up talking for three hours. From that day on, they were rarely apart. Drawn together by their mutual love for the Lord and a desire to go into the mission field together, they became inseparable. Within two months, they knew someday they would be married, and they even began to talk seriously about engagement. All their fellow believers looked up to them as a wonderful example of a godly relationship.

One evening, passion unexpectedly overcame common sense, and the next thing they knew, they were waking up in bed together, stunned by what they had allowed themselves to do.

Suddenly their beautiful, exciting relationship became awkward and strained. Their joy in talking about the Lord vanished. Their mutual passion for the mission field faded as well. Todd was riddled with gut-twisting shame. For the first time in his life, he felt like a failure. He was no longer a confident student and Christian leader. He felt unworthy of God's love and unqualified for leadership. He dropped out of all his church activities. He pulled away from friendships. His grades began to slip. He fell into a deep depression, convinced he'd ruined not only his life and future but Karly's as well.

As for Karly, she was hurt and confused by Todd's behavior. She had thought he loved her. She had made the mistake of giving him her most precious gift—her virginity—but now he was distant and cold toward her. She was full of guilt. When she thought of all her childhood dreams of walking down the aisle in a white wedding gown, symbolizing her purity, she felt sick. She could never hope to have a beautiful love story with Todd now. She had ruined her chance. She was inwardly miserable and had no one to talk to about her pain.

❦

Sadly, these stories reflect the rule rather than the exception in modern Christianity. The vast majority of young people who have grown up in church have allowed some form of sexual compromise into their lives or have had their innocence stripped away by someone else. Eric and I hear countless stories of heartache, regret, and despair from people who feel their lives have been completely ruined in this area. Just in the two days that I've been writing this section, I have had long conversations with two different Christian young women who both grew up with the vision of having a pure, God-written love story, but somewhere along the line, things went wrong. Both of them gave their hearts, minds, and bodies fully to guys who only wanted to use them. One ended up pregnant before she even graduated from high school, and the other is emotionally devastated and unable to forgive herself.

As we discussed earlier, the problem of sexual sin is so rampant in the modern American church that many people are reinterpreting the Bible to downplay the importance of purity. God has an amazing remedy for those wounded by sexual sin. But contrary to popular belief, it's not just giving us a big hug and telling us, "Don't worry, sexual sin is no big deal to Me. I love you anyway." God does love us—so much that He aches to see the tragic problems caused by misuse of His gift of sex. Before we can fully comprehend the hope and restoration He offers, we must first understand the seriousness with which He views sin.

Sin Is Serious

Sexual sin…impurity…moral compromise. In any form, in any circumstance, its effects are devastating. Sin rips lives and hearts apart, destroying innocence, beauty, and joy. Sin's consequences often follow us for the rest of our lives, and sometimes even the next generation must pay the price for the mess we have made.

The most damaging result of sin is that it pushes us away from our Creator. We carry the guilt of what we've done in our hearts, attempting to keep it hidden from Him, and then we end up wandering helpless and alone, miles away from the One who loves us.

Growing up in Christian circles, I observed the issue of sexual sin being treated lightly. In some youth groups I belonged to, it was expected that most of us would give away our virginity before we got married. The attitude was, "You are all going to mess up in this area, because in this day and age, sexual sin is nearly inevitable. But don't worry, God offers a second virginity. His grace will cover you."

There is some truth to that statement. Yes, we will all make mistakes, but this does not mean it is inevitable that we will all fall into sexual sin, or that purity is impossible and that we are just "victims of the culture" if we cannot achieve it. Yes, God *does* offer grace and forgiveness, and He *can* give us a "second virginity," spiritually speaking. But we should never take advantage of His grace. And we should never treat sexual sin lightly. In the eyes of a holy God, all sin is detestable.

When Eric was a young, zealous fireball, traveling the world as a missionary, he was asked to speak at a large youth event in Virginia. As he prayed before the meeting, he felt that God wanted him to speak about purity—spiritual, emotional, and physical. During his talk, he exhorted the young people to live according to God's standards for purity rather than imitating the culture around them. He talked about physical purity, mental purity, and emotional purity. His message was convicting and powerful. And the church leaders did not like it. A youth pastor got up immediately after Eric finished speaking and took the microphone.

"Well, *I'm* not going to preach to you about holiness," he said apologetically, as if preaching "holiness" were as distasteful and inappropriate as giving a lecture on parasite removal from the large intestine.

Afterward, a group of leaders confronted Eric.

"How dare you make all these kids feel condemned. Almost all of them have blown it in the area of purity! It's too sensitive of a subject for you to speak about that way. Now they are going to feel guilty!"

When we take this attitude toward sexual sin—that it's just a little mistake most of us make and that we shouldn't get too hung up on it—we deny the awesome power of what Christ did for us on the Cross. In truth, sexual sin is horrifying. It breaks the heart of God. It destroys that natural, perfect order of love God created between a man and woman. It violates us. We *should* feel remorse when we sin in this way…and we should realize the *gravity* of what we have done. Or if we've been violated by someone else, we should know that God shares in our grief. And yet, that's not where it should end.

Once, after a seminar, Eric knelt to pray with a young man of about twenty-five, who was weeping uncontrollably. His body shook with heartrending sobs. Eric prayed for God's peace to comfort his heart. As he began to calm down, he haltingly revealed to Eric his burden.

"I have given away the most sacred thing I had—my purity. There's nothing left of my treasure. How could I do such a thing? I barely even knew the girl. Now I have nothing to offer my wife. It's too late for me. God doesn't want to waste His time with me anymore. I've ruined my whole life."

Yet before the evening was over, this young man had an encounter with the grace of God, and he was changed. His face became happy and peaceful. He knew he was forgiven.

Another time after a speaking event in Texas, I met a young woman who was nearly numb with guilt and horror over what she had done. Not only had she compromised herself sexually, but she'd also had an abortion. Her eyes were hollow with pain. Yet as she came face to face with her God that day, she became new. When she left, there was a bright sparkle in her eyes. She could begin to move on with her life and discover all God had for her. She knew she was forgiven.

> *I have full confidence that God not only can but delights to forgive me for all of the mistakes I have made in the past. He's given me everything I need to walk in faithfulness and righteousness from the moment I turned to Him. I no longer carry the burdens of guilt and shame because I trust in His strength and He has set me free.*
>
> COURTNEY S., AGE 21

His Tender Smile

The beauty of a God-written love story is not something reserved for the perfect and pious; it's for sinners like you and like me. That's what God's love is all about. We are so unworthy of His grace and forgiveness—and yet He offers it to us freely. If you have fallen in this area of your life and asked yourself the question, "Is it too late for me?" then let the following story from Scripture show you Jesus's heart for *you*, a sinner.

Jesus went to the Mount of Olives. At dawn He came back to the temple, and all the people came to Him. Just as He sat down to teach, the scribes and Pharisees led in a woman who had been caught committing adultery. They made her stand in the middle of everyone.

"Teacher," they said to Him, "this woman has been caught in the very act of committing adultery. In the Law, Moses commanded to stone this kind of woman. What do You say?"…

But Jesus knelt and wrote down something on the ground. As they continued questioning Him, He straightened up and said to them, "The one among you who is without sin, let him throw the first stone at her."

Again, He knelt and wrote down something on the ground. Those who heard left one at a time, beginning with the older ones first, leaving Jesus alone with the woman.[1]

How did Jesus look at the woman who had broken His heart by her sin? In his book *The Parable of Joy*, Michael Card beautifully describes the way Jesus responded to the woman at that moment. The following scene is a perfect portrayal of the tender heart of the Shepherd toward His little lost lambs.

She was standing alone, shivering, in front of the man who was just getting to His feet.

"Where did everyone go?" He asked, smiling. "Didn't anyone condemn you?"

"No," she whispered, looking down. "No one, Sir."

He took her chin in one of His hands. "I don't condemn you either," He said with a tender smile.

Then He became serious. He spoke as a parent disciplining a child. "Now go, and stop sinning."

She began to weep, not from shame as before, but from relief. He had saved her life. He had returned to her what the others…had stolen. She was sorry, painfully sorry. At last she had found Someone who could bear her sorrow for her.[2]

In *The Parable of Joy,* Michael Card notes that author and minister Frederick Buechner once said of Jesus's response to the woman caught in adultery, "He did not condemn her, because He would be condemned *for* her."[3]

Just as Jesus knew the sins of each person in that crowd, He knows every sin we have ever committed from the day we were born. It is pointless to try to hide our sins from Him. Yet when we come to Him, truly broken over what we have done, filled with the soul-piercing regret of realizing how far we have fallen, and we look into His eyes, He smiles tenderly. He lifts our chin with His nail-scarred hand. And He gently says, "I don't condemn you. Now go, and stop sinning."

When we come face to face with this perfect love, it takes our breath away. We deserve to die for what we have done. We should be stoned by an angry mob. Yet not only does Jesus save our life with His own blood, He washes us *completely* clean. When He looks at us, He doesn't see our failures and mistakes; He sees a new creation—a child of God.

He exhorts us to "go, and stop sinning." He is speaking of repentance. The only way we can truly experience the breathtaking love and restoration of God is when we truly repent and become broken over our sin. Shrugging it off and saying, "Sorry I messed up, God, but I'm glad you love me anyway" doesn't cut it. Repentance is the act of humbling ourselves, confessing our sin, and determining in our heart to turn and walk away from our sin from this day forward. True repentance literally means *turning from our sin and walking in the other direction.*

> *Leave the Irreparable Past in His hands, and step out into the Irresistible Future with Him.*[4]
>
> OSWALD CHAMBERS

If we allow Him full and complete access to our lives, He gives us the power to repent, walk a different direction…and be made new. When we repent and accept His forgiveness, He can take the sin our Enemy meant to use to destroy us and instead use it for His glory. He can take a shattered heart and life and script a beautiful tale of His perfect love. As it says in Psalm 103:2–5:

Bless the LORD, O my soul, and forget not all His benefits:
Who forgives all your iniquities, Who heals all your diseases;
Who redeems your life from destruction, Who crowns you with
lovingkindness and tender mercies; who satisfies your mouth
with good things, so that your youth is renewed like the eagle's.

The Power to Forgive

Sexual sin causes pain. To move on to the beautiful plans God has for our lives, we must get past the crippling effects of unforgiveness. Todd cannot forgive himself for falling into sin. Karly cannot forgive herself or Todd for allowing this to happen. Rebecca cannot forgive Jason for destroying her innocence.

When we look straight into the tender, forgiving eyes of our Redeemer, only then do we gain the power to forgive ourselves—and those who have used us. In light of the forgiveness Christ has offered us, how can we offer less to those who have hurt us? As Paul says, "Be kind to one another, tenderhearted, forgiving one another, even as God in Christ forgave you" (Ephesians 4:32).

If you have been devastated by sin, riddled with guilt over your mistakes, or overcome with bitterness toward someone who has used you, run into the arms of Jesus and look into His loving eyes. Allow Him to wash you clean, white as snow, and give you a fresh start. His plans for you are more amazing than you can imagine. Your God-written love story may be just over the horizon! Allow Him to remove

I was sexually abused when I was younger, and I was hurting and ashamed of it, thinking that it was something I had done. I was also very bitter and even hateful toward the people who wronged me. I realized that when I was unwilling to forgive those who sinned against me, it hindered God's work in me! He taught me how to forgive, because He had already forgiven me for all sins I'd ever committed. ...He asked me if I would allow Him to fulfill His promise in Romans 8:28, to work all things for good in my life. So I put my hand in His and He has now used my story to help other girls come to healing and a deeper love for Christ!

ERIKA, AGE 24

the lament of loneliness and remorse you have been singing, and to place into your heart a new song—the "sweeter song."

Remember that once God has forgiven you, it is done. It is finished. To doubt His forgiveness is to doubt whether His work on the Cross was truly enough to cover your sin. Paul tells us to forget what lies behind and press on toward the things that are ahead (Philippians 3:13). As Corrie ten Boom says, God casts our sin into the depths of the sea, and then He posts a sign that reads No Fishing Allowed![5] Don't allow the Enemy to throw condemnation at you for past sin that has already been forgiven by Christ. Once you repent, your sin is nailed to the Cross and it is no longer a part of you. When God looks at you, He doesn't see you as tainted by that sin. In fact, He doesn't see it at all; He's removed it as far away from you as the east is from the west (Psalm 103:12).

No matter what sinful or painful experiences have marred your life in the past, don't buy the Enemy's lie that you are stuck with a second-rate love story. If that were true, Eric and I never would have experienced a God-written love story. When you offer Jesus Christ full and complete access to your heart and life, He makes all things new. Full and complete restoration and a brand-new beginning—that's what the power of His blood can do.

White as Snow

Ten years ago I sat down at my piano and wrote a song called "White as Snow." I composed this song for every young person who is filled with remorse and regret over sexual sin, anyone who is ready to be made new by Christ's redeeming love.

Alone and confused, your heart is bruised from sin;

Your joy is gone from love gone wrong

And you're longing to start again.

I know that you've been hurt, and you don't know who to trust;

I won't pretend I understand your pain.

But I can see repentance in your eyes, and I know it's not too
    late;

I hear Him calling your name…

White as snow, He has made you white as snow;

The moment you confessed, His heart forgave.

You might think you've ruined all the plans He had for you,

But it's for that very reason Jesus saves.

White as snow, He has made you white as snow;

Pure and innocent like a dove,

Though you have done nothing to deserve His pardoning,

You've been purified by Jesus's blood—

White as snow.

The guilt and the shame, keeping you chained,

Not wanting to let you go;

It's not how you dreamed, not how you planned,

And you can't see that still there is hope.

Receive His healing for your bruises;

Receive His riches for your rags.

You cannot imagine all the plans He has for you,

So take His hand, and don't look back.

Therefore I say to you, her sins, which are many, are forgiven, for
she loved much. But to whom little is forgiven, the same loves little.

LUKE 7:47

Those who are well have no need of a physician, but those
who are sick. I did not come to call the righteous, but sinners,
to repentance.

MARK 2:17

A Look Inside Your Heart

1. In what ways has your life been touched by sexual sin?
   How has this affected your view of yourself? of God?
2. Why do you suppose our culture glosses over sexual sin as
   if it's no big deal?
3. How would your view of yourself change if you could look
   into Jesus's eyes and know that He sees only a new creation,
   a precious child of God?
4. If you're harboring guilt and condemnation over the past,
   are you willing to allow Christ to wash you completely
   clean? Are you ready to truly repent of your sin, turning to
   walk in the other direction and relying on the enabling
   power of God for victory from this day forward?

A Step Further

As you process the truths you've read in this chapter, now is the perfect time to quietly steal away and kneel before the throne of God.

Read through Psalm 51 and let the words of David begging his Lord for forgiveness become the cry of your heart to God. Then read Luke 15:11–24 and let yourself go on a journey with the wayward son. Allow the loving and welcoming arms of your Father to enfold you and take you back once again. Write down all that He whispers to your heart. Then make a choice to walk in His glorious forgiveness and freedom from this day forward, relying on His strength to keep your eyes looking straight ahead and not backwards. ✕

Fifteen

Against the Tide

*Gaining real backbone in the midst
of a spineless generation*

✕ ERIC ✕

The night air was frigid cold. In the dark, icy prison cell sat two young Chinese men, emaciated from loss of food and light. They had only one thin blanket between the two of them to protect against the freezing cold.

The hard floor beneath them was cruel and merciless, and the shackles around their ankles seemed to mock their pain. Yet in this arctic sanctuary of doom was heavenly warmth.

One of the two young men had a thought.

If that were Jesus next to me, would I give Him my blanket?

This Chinese man, who had nothing but a thin blanket to keep himself warm, recognized the privilege it would be to give what little he had to the God who had given him *everything*. He removed the blanket from around his shoulders and placed it around the shoulders of his shivering friend.

Our Blanket, Our Life

Picture yourself in the same icy-cold prison cell. Imagine you are thin and frail and trembling from the cold. All you have is a thin blanket to warm yourself. How tightly would you cling to the little comfort you have? What would it take for you to part with your precious blanket?

You see, that thin blanket represents your life. If you give up your blanket, you are going to die. If you let go of your lone security, you must surrender to death.

But what if the person next to you in that cell was Jesus? What if you had the privilege of giving what little you had to the one who gave up His life for you? What if you *really did* have the opportunity to show your love and gratitude to the King of all kings and the Creator of the universe? Would you give up your blanket?

As a generation, we have been taught to hold on to our blankets—to take charge of our lives and secure our future even at the expense of

The covenant with our King is a solemn vow. It's a covenant that reaches into eternity. We remember it every time we take communion. . . . By taking the bread and the wine, we are saying, "I remember, cherish, and praise You, Jesus Christ, for the Life You have given me. And today I also remember that I am Yours, completely and unreservedly. My body is for You to break, and my blood is for You to pour out as You see fit."[1]

ERIC LUDY, *GOD'S GIFT TO WOMEN*

those around us. But we fail to realize that the security of our future rests not in our blankets, but in Jesus sitting next to us. When we choose to give instead of keep, we discover a little taste of heaven on earth. When we choose to let go of what little we have and surrender it to God, then we receive the bounty of His kingdom.

Our love-hungry generation is desperately searching for the "beautiful side of love." But it is not found in either having sex or abstaining from sex. The "sweeter song" is Jesus, in all His fullness, all His love, all His beauty, all His grace, and all His majesty.

When you know Jesus Christ, the tender hand of heaven begins to masterfully shape your life to exhibit the glory of heaven for the entire world to see. When you know the Great Author of romance, the tender hand of heaven takes you by the heart and trains you to love as the Great Lover Himself. He trains you to be patient and pure. He trains you to be tender and true. With Jesus at the center of your life, you not only gain blissful hope for the here and now but unquenchable excitement for the eternity before you.

The sweeter song is sung on a ship that is headed against the tide. Its course is charted to go directly into the headwinds. Jesus plays the sweetest melody men's ears have ever heard, but you need backbone to board the ship on which it is played.

Many churches give off the vibe that Christianity is cool, perhaps hoping that more people would become Christians if they knew that churches weren't full of brainless idiots who lean on God as a crutch because they can't handle life's problems on their own. Well, in heaven Christianity is cool, but here on earth Christianity is anything but cool. Followers of true Christianity throughout history have been mocked and ridiculed, persecuted and even killed by the world. In fact, anyone who chooses to truly live like Christ in this world will undoubtedly meet the same fate: the cross.

Christianity is not the easy way to pass through this life. To hear the tender melody line of the sweeter song requires a sacrifice! Often it means losing your reputation, being misunderstood by the masses… or even giving up your thin blanket— letting go of your life.

> *The man who has God for his treasure has all things in One.*[2]
>
> A. W. TOZER

I have a vision for this younger generation of Christians. I want to see us go beyond Sunday morning services and Wednesday night Bible studies and learn to love Christ in every minute of every day. I want to see us go beyond just memorizing Scripture and knowing the verbiage of the Bible to actually having our lives transformed by its amazing Truth, so that we don't just know it but we live it for all the world to witness. I want to see us fight to protect the beautiful side of love in our romantic relationships so that we can bring glory to the Great Lover of our souls.

Many have commented on how the younger generation lacks leaders. And many have said if we don't change course, we're headed straight for the rocks upon which the Sirens sit. And unfortunately, I would have to agree. In general, this is a dying, spineless generation. We lack the courage to stand for anything that's politically and socially incorrect. We lack the faith to trust that God is as perfect and powerful as He says He is. We lack the fire to *pursue* God, the zeal to *know* God, and the humility to *allow* God to do whatever He pleases with our lives.

We live in a world inundated with sexual perversity, overwhelmed with relational infidelity, and marked by a skyrocketing number of divorces and plummeting marriage rates. When I think how desperately we need young leaders to stand up, I am reminded of a heroic tale that unfolded on the Judean countryside many thousands of years ago.

Seeing Beyond the Hulk

All hope seemed lost. The odds were heavily favoring the champion. After all, who could possibly beat him? He was huge! He was stronger than an ox and as big as a small dinosaur. His biceps alone could have housed a small family. Not only that, but he had the attitude needed to win a fight like this one. Sportswriters today call it cocky; back then they just called it "Whoa, Momma! I'm not gonna fight this dude!"

The ring was not in Caesars Palace, but actually in a less glittery venue called the Valley of Elah. And this wasn't a fight to the ten count, but a fight to the death. This wasn't a fight for fame, but a fight for the future of a nation. This showdown was one for the history books before the bell even rang.

Each nation chose its fighter. It was the Hulk, weighing in at five hundred-plus pounds and able to swallow a baby tiger with a single gulp, against the Kid, a young shepherd about the same size as the champion's left leg. The Hulk howled with laughter as he saw the Kid stroll out to fight.

If a nation's future hung in the balance, why choose a shepherd boy to fight for you? Why not pick your greatest warrior to match strength with the champion? The odds were already a million to one. Why make them even worse?

Well, this nation picked its fighter based not on public opinion polls or in alignment with the odds, but because he was the only one willing to fight. Every other warrior was quaking in his combat boots.

But don't judge the Kid on his external size and physical prowess. The Kid was special! He knew something that every other warrior in his entire nation had yet to learn. He knew that when you stand up for God, He stands up for you.

The Hulk was mocking God and His people. Only this unimpressive Kid seemed to believe that no one gets away with something like that. So he said, "I'll take him on!"

> *God has ventured all in Jesus Christ to save us, now He wants us to venture our all in abandoned confidence in Him.*[3]
>
> OSWALD CHAMBERS

I'm convinced that when the Kid strolled out to meet the Hulk that day, it wasn't the awesome size, the impenetrable strength, and the death-defying confidence of the giant he saw. I believe he saw his infinitely enormous and all-powerful God standing behind the scrawny giant, with His gargantuan fist over the Hulk's miniuscule head, saying to the young shepherd, "Just tell me when!" *CRUNCH!!*

The Kid's name was David. And he was a leader in a generation that only had eyes for the "Hulk" named Goliath (see 1 Samuel 17). He was fearless amid a generation that trembled with fear. And he was a man who showed backbone when surrounded by quivering, spineless peers.

We desperately need Davids in our generation. We need leaders who will trust God implicitly. We need men and women who will

You've trusted Jesus with your life, now live that life in Him. Inhaling Him. Exhaling Him. Making Him your life-source each and every day with the faith of a little child! You were planted in the richest of soils and watered with the amazing Truth of His Kingdom. Don't hide the joy-filled life of Jesus beneath the soil, but grow and bloom for all the world to see.

COLOSSIANS 2:7 (PARAPHRASE)

stand up against the "hulks" in our culture and not back down. We need heroes who will not pattern their lives after the fearful throng around them but after the courage of Christ.

It's time we found some ordinary people who choose to love God in extraordinary ways.

What About *Your* Blanket?

Join me, once again, in that icy prison cell. Place yourself on that mercilessly hard floor, and remember that you are frigidly cold. That thin blanket represents your only comfort, your only blockade from the deathly chill.

Imagine that it is not a young Chinese man shivering next to you, but your future spouse. Then ask yourself the question, *If that were Jesus seated next to me, would I give Him my blanket?*

As you ponder how you would respond, maybe you hold up your blanket and see that it is tattered and torn. Maybe you don't even have a blanket left. The decisions you've made up to this point have unraveled your life until all that remains is a mere thread that drapes itself across your heart, attempting to protect you from the bitter cold.

Many of us don't even have much of a blanket to offer the spouse who's shivering beside us. But if we were to see that person as Jesus, would we be willing to give the little we *do* have to the God who gave us so much, trusting Him to weave something new and beautiful out of the frayed remains?

Extravagant love, as in every generation before us, has been ridiculed and scorned. It is seen as wasteful and reckless overspending. But extravagant love—the offering of everything, the emptying of the pockets of our life—is the essence of true Christianity. It was extravagant love that caused Jesus to give up His throne in heaven and give us the gift of life at the expense of His own. It was extravagant love that compelled the Chinese Christian to sacrifice his only source of warmth for the benefit of his brother in prison. And it would be extravagant love that would rouse you to take the blanket off your shoulders today and wrap it around the shoulders of your worthy King.

If you allow the tender hand of heaven to pour this kind of extravagant love into your heart, then you will truly be ready to be a successful lover. With an extravagant love stirring in your every attitude and action, it is fairly certain you will not be applauded by this world, but the heavenly hosts will be on their feet cheering as you model the beautiful side of love for the entire universe.

Be assured, if you walk with Him and look to Him and expect help from Him, He will never fail you.[4]

GEORGE MUELLER

When you entrust the "pen" of your life to the Great Author of romance and learn how to love with extravagance—how to give away your life in loving another—you won't just be humming the praises of God for a lifetime, but you will be singing the sweeter song for all eternity!

As Oswald Chambers said, "If we deliberately choose to obey God, then He will tax the remotest star and the last grain of sand to assist us with all His almighty power."[5]

A Final Challenge

Our loving Savior and Lord has given us a fantastic opportunity: to rise above the watered-down version of love this world offers and take hold of the truest and most lasting kind of love imaginable. It's a chance to set aside Hollywood's sappy standards and discover romance at its best—the romance of heaven! It's time to make a choice. We can embrace an empty, selfish lifestyle that ends in heartache and despair, or we can learn to live and love selflessly...just like our own Great Lover Himself.

God is longing to write *your* love story—a love story far beyond the most incredible fairy tale ever written. Will you give Him the pen today?

You cannot stay the way you are and go with God.[6]

HENRY BLACKABY

The thing that taxes almightiness is the very thing which we as disciples of Jesus ought to believe He will do.[7]

OSWALD CHAMBERS

Whoever of you does not forsake all that he has cannot be My disciple.

LUKE 14:33

And he who does not take his cross and follow after Me is not worthy of Me.

MATTHEW 10:38

A Look Inside Your Heart

1. Have you ever faced criticism because of a decision to truly live like Christ? If so, describe the situation.
2. What, if anything, about your life right now suggests you're walking a different path than this culture?
3. In what specific areas have you simply gone along with the culture and need to gain more of a backbone?
4. Are you ready to give Him the pen to write not only your love story, but your entire life story as well? If so, how will you confirm that decision in a tangible way today?

A Step Further

Take some time to read through the amazing account in Daniel 6:4–23. Then go on a little stroll and invite Jesus to come along. As you walk, ponder the world in which you live. God has placed you on this earth for such a time as this. Let this day be a turning point in your life—make a decision to stand against the tide for His Truth. You cannot do this in your own strength, but if you remember the enormous God who is backing you up, you will be filled with true courage to face the giants. He will never leave you (see Hebrews 13:5). Write down your commitment to stand for Him, and then pray for His enabling power to back you up from this moment on. ✕

After "I Do"

The beauty of a God-written marriage

✕ LESLIE ✕

My love story with Eric was beyond any fairy-tale romance I had ever imagined. Our wedding was a breathtaking taste of heaven on earth. Our honeymoon was perfect—two weeks of ethereal bliss. We rode away into the sunset to live happily ever after.

And then came the fleas.

And the noisy family of raccoons in our chimney.

And the subzero temperatures that made our car break down constantly.

And the broken pipes that flooded our kitchen at 3:00 a.m.

And my six-week bout with severe bronchitis.

Two months into our marriage, our life looked like anything *but* a beautiful fairy tale come true.

As with many young couples, finances were tight. We lived in a rented house in Michigan, miles away from the nearest city. In the

summer, the house was used as a bed-and-breakfast for tourists, surrounded by gorgeous flowers and beautiful trees overlooking a shim-
mering lake. But in the heart of winter, when *we* lived there, it was a
different story. The lake was frozen. The skies were gloomy. The trees
were barren. The house seemed eerie and isolated, like the setting for
a horror film.

Whenever Eric was at work, I became desperately lonely. I was
alone in the huge creepy house all day long, without a car and without a job. Since I had just moved to Michigan, I knew very few people
in the area. We had no neighbors nearby. I missed my family. I missed
my friends. I missed my life back in Colorado.

But that was only the beginning of my woes.

"I think there might be bedbugs in our mattress," I announced to
Eric one morning, scratching a patch of red bumps that had surfaced
on my leg.

The house had seven bedrooms, so that night we tried sleeping in
a different bed. But when morning came, I had even more red spots
than before. Eric, too, began to notice a few itchy marks on his legs.
After a week of trying out every bed in the place, we were only getting
more and more covered with the strange bites. We washed the bed-
ding, vacuumed the mattresses, and scrutinized each bed for bedbugs,
but we never came any closer to solving the mystery.

Then one day my eye caught an unusual movement on the living
room floor. Crouching down, I saw hundreds of tiny black spots, leaping up and down out of the carpet fibers. Our bites weren't from bedbugs; they were from *fleas*.

The house was infested.

Horrified, I called Eric at work and told him to pick up a can of flea killer on his way home. That night we set off a super-potent "flea bomb" that the hardware store clerk assured us would kill every flea within a two-mile radius.

The clerk was wrong.

The next day, the fleas seemed to have multiplied. All day long, they attacked me with a new vengeance. No matter where I sat in the house, within minutes my clothes would be covered with at least fifty of the disgusting insects. By this time, my arms and legs looked as if I had fallen asleep in a patch of poison ivy.

We sprayed again. And once more, the fleas seemed to thrive on the high-octane bugkiller that now permeated the air.

To make matters worse, that night I woke up with a pounding headache, coughing loud enough to rattle the windows. I was having an allergic reaction to the flea bombs.

The subzero weather, mixed with the harsh chemicals that filled the house, began to take a toll on my body. What started as a fit of coughing developed quickly into an alarming case of bronchitis. The doctor prescribed a regimen of antibiotics and bed rest. Within a week I had gone through an entire supply closet full of Kleenex boxes.

I was lonely, sicker than I had been in years, and covered in flea-bites. I was sure things couldn't get any worse.

I was wrong.

One morning, as I lay on the couch shaking with fever, I heard strange noises coming from the fireplace. Someone or something was scratching and rustling around inside the brick walls, just three feet away from me. It sounded like a very large animal. My heart began pulsating with fear as visions of vicious wolves and wild bears filled my head. Not that a bear could fit into the chimney, but I think my fever was making me a bit irrational.

The fireplace had no cover except a thin board propped against the opening to keep out cold drafts. My eyes froze on the sparse piece of lumber—the only barrier between me and the unseen intruder. And as I watched in terror, the board moved. The unwelcome visitor was pushing against it, trying to get into the house! Suddenly, the tip of a sharp black claw poked through a small hole in the wood.

Trying to keep from screaming, I grabbed an armchair and wrestled it in front of the board. Then I snatched up a fireplace poker and sat poised, ready to fight whatever savage animal was about to break in and attack me. I waited there for an hour. The creature eventually gave up its pursuit, and the clawing noises finally died down. But my heart didn't slow its rapid hammering for the rest of the day.

The animal in the fireplace turned out to be a raccoon. In fact, an entire *family* of raccoons had decided to spend the winter in our chimney. Having grown up in suburbia, I was basically a wimp when it came to wildlife. I began to have nightmares of the raccoons pushing down the board, bursting into the house, and chasing me around the room with their razor-sharp teeth. We tried many methods of extracting the raccoons, from setting traps to smoking them out, but like the fleas, nothing seemed to chase them away.

One night, in the middle of another terrifying raccoon dream in which I lost three fingers and contracted rabies, I woke to the sound of a loud waterfall cascading through the kitchen. Eric and I rushed downstairs to find icy water spraying everywhere. The laundry room pipes had burst from the record-breaking cold.

Three hours later, after Eric's daring venture into the pitch-black, spider-infested crawlspace under the house, the exploded pipe had stopped spraying water, the mess was cleaned up, and our washing machine was officially declared broken. As if we needed another trial.

In the space of a month, we'd been attacked by fleas, haunted by raccoons, plagued by sickness, stressed by financial challenges, and inconvenienced by a car that always seemed to die at the worse possible time. Now this? Though both of us had attempted to maintain a positive attitude, our spirits were seriously sagging.

A few days later, Eric came home to find me lying on the couch, too sick to move. Piles of Kleenex and dirty laundry littered the floor. The raccoons scratched and clawed in the fireplace. Outside, gusts of wind and snow swirled around the dismal winter terrain. I had spent the day in utter misery, rotating between coughing fits and scratching attacks.

"I can't believe just a month ago we were in Phoenix, lying by the pool and sipping strawberry lemonade," I lamented wearily, longing to return to our recent days of honeymoon bliss.

Eric sank heavily into a chair beside me. "I didn't want our first few weeks of marriage to be this way," he told me regretfully. "I am so sorry, Les."

"It's not your fault," I reminded him, trying to sound cheerful.

We sat for a few moments in dejected silence. Suddenly, Eric looked at me thoughtfully.

"I think there's something we need to do," he said. "We've been clinging to our own hopes and expectations for the way our life together was supposed to turn out. We've been so focused on trying to figure out why things aren't happening the way we planned that we haven't stopped to give the pen to God. We need to let Him script this next chapter of our life."

We knelt together on the flea-infested rug. Once again, we surrendered our plans, dreams, and desires to the loving Author of romance. Our Lord had perfectly scripted our love story, and now we were asking Him to script each detail of our *life* story as we began the adventure of marriage.

As we entrusted our pen to Him, my heart instantly flooded with an overwhelming sense of peace and fulfillment. Our Lord had never been anything but faithful to us, and I knew He wouldn't stop now.

"Do with our lives whatever You will, Lord," I prayed sincerely. "Even if that means living with fleas and raccoons forever, I am willing."

And so the pattern began again. The Author of romance took our pen and began scripting an amazing tale for our life together. And in fourteen years of marriage, He has never let us down.

Those who declare, "Romance dies after the honeymoon!" have obviously never experienced the beauty of a God-written marriage.

Have things always been easy for us? Absolutely not. In fact, the fleas and raccoons turned out to be an insignificant trial in comparison with some of the intense storms that Eric and I have weathered over the years. We have experienced tremendous disappointment, discouragement, stress, and physical challenges in our journey together.

But with Christ at the center of our relationship, the hard times have only strengthened our commitment and deepened our love for each other.

Even now, we sometimes find ourselves taking that pen back—clinging too tightly to our own plans or expectations. That's when we are reminded to fall to our knees and surrender the pen to our faithful God one more time.

When He scripts each detail of our story, life becomes an endless frontier of adventure. In the good times and the bad, marriage is a glorious taste of heaven when the Author of romance holds the pen.

Faithfully

Lyrics by Eric and Leslie Ludy

Tonight I saw a shooting star,
Made me wonder where you are.
For years I have been dreaming of you,
And I wonder if you're thinking of me, too.

In this world of cheap romance
And love that only fades after the dance,
They say that I'm a fool to wait for something more.
How can I really love someone I've never seen before?

But I have longed for true love every day that I have lived,
And I know real love is all about learning how to give.
So I pray that God will bring you to me,
And I pray you'll find me waiting faithfully.

CHORUS
Faithfully, I am yours
From now until forever.
Faithfully, I will write,
Write you a love song with my life.
'Cause this kind of love's worth waiting for
No matter how long it takes.
I am yours
Faithfully

Tonight I saw two lovers kiss,
Reminded me of my own loneliness.
They say that I'm a fool to keep on praying for you.
How can I give up pleasure for a dream that won't come true?

But I will keep believing that God still has a plan.
And though I cannot see you now, I know that He can,
And someday I will give you all of me.
Until I find you, I'll be waiting faithfully.

Relationship Q&A

Answers to common questions about guy/girl stuff

✕ ERIC ✕

Over the years Leslie and I have been asked countless relationship questions. In the following pages you'll find our answers to some of the most common dilemmas young adults face in guy/girl relationships. For answers to some of the tougher questions regarding sexuality, such as physical boundaries in pre-marriage relationships, homosexuality, lust and pornography, oral sex, masturbation, and more, please read our book *Meet Mr. Smith*.

1. Is it wrong to date?

When I think of the word *date* I always think of a piece of fruit—and it's not a particularly attractive piece of fruit, mind you. *Date* is a funny word, and a rather ugly word. In fact, this one word *date* has posed some of my greatest challenges in working with young people over the past decade.

"So, Eric, are you saying I'm not supposed to date?"

No, you are not the first one to have that thought flit through your mind while reading this book. It's surprisingly common. So, since everyone is thinking it, why don't we spend a few moments to answer that wonderful question.

Yes, it is only four letters long, but the word *date* holds within it a million shades of meaning and a thousand possible definitions. The answer to the question, "Is it wrong to date?" all hinges on which definition of *date* we are working from.

To much of the modern world, "to date" means "to engage in an exclusive sexual relationship with someone prior to marriage." Well, by that definition, wouldn't you agree that the practice of dating falls outside the pale of appropriate, Christ-born pre-marriage behavior? However, what if your definition of dating is two families getting together for beef stroganoff and a young man from one family and a young woman from another family both sheepishly shuffling their feet as they talk about the weather? Sounds quite harmless to me.

For most Christians, the definition of dating falls somewhere between sexual hookups and dinner with friends, which is why this question poses so many problems.

If your notion of dating is born of the prime-time sitcom mentality—the "love who you are with, sleep with who you are with" sort of thinking—then without hesitation I would state, "Yes, it is wrong to date!" However, if your idea of dating is sheepishly shuffling feet while surrounded by your little brother, Mom, and cousin Larry, then I would venture to say dating doesn't pose much of a risk.

Personally, I don't care for the word *date*. I think it diminishes the grandeur of a God-written love story into a common, everyday sort of thing. If you are stuck on using the word, I won't fight you. But I prefer to think that God's version of love and romance is miles above the culturally saturated ideas contained within that weak and ugly word.

When two people enter into a relationship that is scripted from start to finish by the Author of love and relationships, they may prefer to view their relationship as something bigger, better, and more beautiful than *dating*.

In short, if you can maintain the honor, the faithfulness of heart, the purity, and the selfless love of Christ at the center of your relationship, go ahead and date. However, if you are holding the pen in your proud hand and messing with a human heart for your selfish pleasure, my advice is, *don't date*; instead, go to Jesus and ask Him to change you and change your method for building an intimate love relationship.

As we've discussed throughout this book, to embrace the true gospel means giving Jesus Christ full access to your life, and that includes your love life. You can trust His way of doing it and you can trust that God's methods for establishing love relationships are a million times bigger, better, and more beautiful than the world's design—and fully worth discarding the ugly word *dating* to find.

2. If I am not part of the typical dating scene, how will I ever get to know someone well enough to begin a relationship?

Our God is a creative God. He doesn't need to imitate the world's way of building a relationship. Our limited human minds so often think that if we don't date around the way everyone else does, we'll never be in a position to find real love. However, the opposite is often true. When you're moving in and out of relationships at your own whim, you aren't giving God the opportunity to bring someone into your life through His own unique and creative means.

Leslie and I got to know each other in an unconventional way.

We spent time together at family gatherings, church functions, and on short-term mission outreaches. We didn't need to be in a dating relationship to become better acquainted. By the time we knew God was leading us toward marriage, we'd still never even been on one "date" with each other. When God puts something together, He orchestrates plenty of opportunities for the friendship to flourish and the relationship to blossom, without needing the typical dating scene to facilitate the process.

Remember Krissy's story? She purposely chose to live in a place where relationship opportunities were scarce and there were hardly any available men because she knew she was where God had called her to be. She left it up to God—and He brought her husband into her life from seemingly out of nowhere, in His own perfect time.

God cares more about this area of your life than even you do. You can trust Him not only to bring your future spouse into your life, but also to provide the opportunity to get to know that person in His own perfect time and way. Just relax and leave it up to Him. You'll be amazed by His creativity and faithfulness!

3. What if I'm currently in a relationship that isn't Christ-centered? Can a love story become God-written once it's started off the wrong way?

God is more interested in the state of our hearts than in the state of our human relationships. Oh, He does care about our relationships, but God isn't in the business of forming healthy human relationships between two people whose souls are dying and twisted by sin.

The first thing we need to do when we realize we are off track is to get right with God. Our question shouldn't be "Can this love story

I'm currently in be somehow salvaged?" but rather, "No matter the cost, how can I get back into a right relationship with my God?"

If you are currently in the midst of a crooked, self-satisfying relationship, then the first step is make sure you give Christ His rightful position moving forward. And (gulp) that may mean you need to end the relationship in which you are currently engaged. That said, our God is a God of redemption, and if He wants your relationship to move forward and thrive, He is perfectly capable of taking what was crooked and self-satisfying and transforming it into something pure, beautiful, and God-glorifying.

Bottom line: God can redeem only that which we hand fully over to Him. If you want your love story to come from His hand, then the relationship you are currently involved in needs to be surrendered. You must allow Him to take it, to dissolve it if necessary, to clean it, purify it, or even to rebuild it from scratch if He so desires. The point is, the relationship must be *His* and no longer your property. Yes, it may need to end, or there may need to be a season of separation in which a healthy foundation can be built. But whatever it may mean, I can assure you that when your love life becomes His, amazing things will happen.

4. The person I'm dating right now doesn't really know God. Should I end the relationship?

As a Christian, your relationship with God is more important than any other relationship. It is impossible to deepen your intimacy with God while simultaneously giving your life to a member of the opposite sex who doesn't share that desire.

Hair color, smile, personality type, height, weight—these social and physical attributes usually dance about in people's minds when they think about who they might wish to one day marry. But none of that matters if Jesus Christ isn't at the very center of a person's soul. Even if you get matched with the nicest or most beautiful person on Planet Earth, if Jesus Christ isn't the primary focal point of that individual's soul, then a God-written love story will not be possible.

If you are involved with an unbeliever, then I would strongly advise you to step back from the relationship and provide an opportunity for this unbeliever to encounter God.

A word of caution: be sure that the person in question doesn't just feign acceptance of Christ in order to win you back. If you make it clear that you are ending the relationship because you don't want to be united with an unbeliever, then it might be tempting for your unbelieving boyfriend or girlfriend to go through the motions of becoming a Christian in order to regain the relationship. When someone becomes a genuine believer in Christ, their lifestyle, motives, conversation, direction, and attitude are remade by Him. So if there seems to be a decision for Christ, let some time pass to make sure it's not just a mental choice but a true life transformation. Also, don't just assume that you should dive right back into a relationship just because the other person is a Christian. Make sure God is truly holding the pen and allow Him to script your story as He sees fit, even if He takes the plotline in a completely new direction!

5. I've already compromised sexually in my current relationship, but we both want to do it God's way from now on. What should we do?

When sexual compromise has been given sway in a couple's relationship, then greater guards must be set up moving forward. First off, I personally would suggest a season of separation in order to allow God to rebuild your individual souls and fortify you with His strength and grace for dealing with lust and sensual bait. Having a season of separation (more than just a couple of days!) helps you to refocus and start fresh. Devote plenty of time to prayer and seeking godly counsel; really pursue God's perspective on the relationship before you dive back in.

If you and your boyfriend or girlfriend have truly repented of sexual sin and feel God is leading you back into a serious relationship headed toward marriage, then be sure to set up stricter protective boundaries than before. Once a couple opens the door to sexual intimacy, they'll feel a strong pull to return to that pattern. You may think that you'll have the willpower to resist temptation, but God reminds us that even the strongest souls are vulnerable to sexual compromise:

> Do not let your heart turn aside to her ways, do not stray into her paths; for she has cast down many wounded, and all who were slain by her were strong men. (Proverbs 7:25–26)

If you choose to enter back into a relationship in which there has already been sexual compromise, set up clear boundaries to help you avoid getting into compromising situations. Establish a clear set of guidelines that you both commit to follow, such as not being alone together, not having erotic conversations, putting strict limits on physical touch, etc. I would also highly recommend having outside accountability partners who frequently ask you specific questions about how the relationship is going, how you are spending your time, and how the issue of sexual temptation stands. If you know that you are going to have to answer to your parents, pastor, brother, close friend, or some other trusted person for the way you handle yourself sexually in the relationship, you will be far less likely to throw caution to the wind in the heat of the moment.

Yes, I know that setting up boundaries such as these can seem far more like rules than the sweeter song. However, if you're willing to do whatever it takes to guard the purity of the relationship and to keep Christ at the center from this day forward, you will discover that your commitment to respecting these boundaries brings beauty, not oppression, to your love story—and sets the stage for a fresh new beginning.

6. There is someone in my life I'm interested in romantically. What should I do?

First of all, don't be in a hurry! So often we feel an urgent need to make something happen before we lose our opportunity. But remember that if God is writing your love story, He will keep everything in place until the time is right. If this person is meant for you, God will not allow him or her to slip away when you slow down and take the time to seek Him rather than rushing into something.

Second, pray! I'm not talking about just a brief mention of the situation in your bedtime prayers, but really taking the time to lay the situation before God, cry out to Him for wisdom, and let Him align your thoughts and desires with His. Even if it takes a few weeks or months of prayer before you have clear direction from God, don't overlook this superimportant step. Only a relationship bathed in prayer from start to finish can truly sparkle with the beauty of heaven. And only when you have genuinely prayed and sought the heart of God will you have the clear wisdom and direction you need to take the next step.

Third, seek godly counsel. Even before taking a step forward, it's a great idea to surround yourself with people who can support you with prayer, advice, and accountability. Recruit some godly teammates to join with you in seeking God's heart for the relationship and His wisdom on how and when to move forward. If you do, you'll have a lot more confidence and a clearer perspective than if you try to swing it on your own.

A note to girls: when Leslie and I reached the stage in our relationship where we both felt that God wanted to do something beyond friendship, we experienced an awkward period of time when our relationship was undefined. I hadn't yet told Leslie that I felt God wanted me to enter into a serious relationship with her, and she was left guessing and wondering about where things stood between us. I was leaving in just a few weeks to go to missionary school, and Leslie felt an acute need to sit down with me and discuss where our friendship was going. But every time she was tempted to initiate a conversation with me, something held her back. She wanted me to be the leader in the relationship; she didn't want to rob me of my masculinity by stepping into the role of initiator. When I finally felt the freedom from God to sit down and share with Leslie that I felt we would one day be married, I told her how much I appreciated her letting me be the "man" in the relationship, allowing me to be the one to initiate the next step between us. I felt honored and respected because she didn't take the lead, even though she found it extremely difficult to wait.

Most young women complain that guys aren't good leaders in a relationship, and many married women wish their husbands would take the reins and be the spiritual and relational leader of the home.

But often that pattern is sabotaged from the very beginning by an impatient woman who robs the guy of the opportunity to be the leader God intended Him to be. As Leslie writes in her book *Set-Apart Femininity*:

> When a woman tries to take a man's role in a relationship, she robs him of his masculine strength. Sure, he may at first appear to like it when a woman pursues him. After all, it saves him the insecurity of sticking his neck out or having to go to the effort of carefully winning her heart. He may be temporarily flattered by her aggression toward him, but in the end, he will lose respect for both her and his own masculinity. Instead of becoming her protector and leader, he will become lazy and lackluster, expecting her to do all the work in the relationship.
>
> On the flip side, if a woman allows a man to rise to the challenge of pursuing her, wooing her, and winning her heart over time, instead of thrusting it upon him too readily, his masculine strength will be tested and strengthened. Once he has pursued and won his prize according to God's perfect pattern, he is far less likely to take her for granted. Rather, he will become the heroic protector he was created to be—laying down his life to preserve and nurture the heart of the princess whom he worked so hard to win.[1]

Guys, the role of initiator falls to you. A man of honor is a man who shoulders the responsibility of being the leader and who carefully and sensitively wins a woman's heart, submitting to the guidance of God's Spirit every step of the way. It's up to you to take the first step in a relationship. But beware of the "bull in a china shop" syndrome. Don't be blunt or aggressive toward a woman the way you would be toward your brother. Rather, be sensitive to how the young woman is feeling about the progress of the relationship. Allow time for her to open her heart to you. Get to know her and show that you are interested in who she is as a person and a child of God rather than simply as a potential wife. Make sure you demonstrate honor and establish trust in the friendship before trying to take the next step. Otherwise, the poor girl may scamper away like a rabbit running from a hound dog.

As in all things, the key is to wait for God's timing and His Spirit's lead; don't just follow your own whims.

7. What do you think about Christian online dating services? I know lots of people who found their soul mate that way. Is it wrong to give it a try?

Maybe this is a personal thing, but the idea of using a Christian online dating service as the catalyst for a lifelong love story seems about as unromantic and unamazing as it gets. I realize that "romantic" and "amazing" may not be at the top of your laundry list when it comes to your love life. In fact, you may be thinking, "It's either cyber-dating, Eric, or I've got nothing!"

Well, you do have God.

Don't get me wrong. I think it's perfectly plausible that two people could meet, fall in love, and build a God-honoring love story in and through the means of an online dating service. However, that being said, it is also perfectly plausible that two people could do the very same thing after meeting at a single's bar. The fact that good things can miraculously emerge out of less-than-perfect places serves more as evidence of a redemptive God than as an endorsement for frequenting less-than-perfect places.

And to be honest, that is how I see online dating services. I don't necessarily put cyber-dating in the same category of hooking up with someone at a single's bar, but it's certainly a less-than-perfect way to go about the process of building a love story. One young woman who recently wrote to Leslie about her experience with a Christian online dating network said, "I felt like I was in the midst of a school of sharks!" Another young man I talked with said, "It was nothing but a meat market."

As both of these individuals discovered, even in "Christian" online dating environments there is plenty of temptation toward emotion-led, humanly manipulated romance, plus there is the added disadvantage of not getting to know someone in a real-life situation. This can open up a lot of opportunities for subtle deception.

It's not that meeting someone through an online dating network can't involve God, and it's not that God can't take the pen in and through that process to script a beautiful tale. However, in the whole scheme of God's intent for romance and relationships, online dating ranks fairly low on the desirability scale. It's simply an underwhelming expression of God's limitless ability in this all-important arena.

God loves to do things in an unpredictable fashion. He loves the marvel and wonder of surprise. He loves the faith-building, character-deepening dependency of waiting and trusting. Remember, He created romance. He knows how to maximize it. If both God and Christian online dating services are in the business of building love stories, I say choose God's rendition; you will not be disappointed.

Notes

Chapter 1

1. Technically it's now supposed to be "Blaine and Barbie," but I still have a soft spot for good old Ken.

Chapter 2

1. Richard Lattimore, *Homer's Odyssey* (New York: Harper and Row, 1950), 189–190.
2. *The Facts on File Encyclopedia of World Mythology and Legend,* s.v. "Orpheus."

Chapter 3

1. John Foxe, *Foxe's Book of Martyrs* (Grand Rapids, MI: Baker, 1990), 7–8.
2. Eric Ludy, *God's Gift to Women* (Colorado Springs: Multnomah, 2003), 106.
3. Henry Clay Trumbull as quoted in Mrs. Charles E. Cowman, *Streams in the Desert* (Grand Rapids, MI: Zondervan, 1984), 31.
4. As quoted in Elisabeth Elliot, *Shadow of the Almighty: The Life and Testament of Jim Elliot* (San Francisco: HarperCollins, 1979), 15.
5. Leonard Ravenhill, from the audio recording "Long Interview of Leonard Ravenhill by David Mainse" at www.sermonindex.net/ modules/mydownloads/singlefile.php?lid=1010.

Chapter 4

1. Oswald Chambers, *My Utmost for His Highest* (Uhrichsville, OH: Barbour Publishing, 1935), 37. This material is taken from *My Utmost for His Highest* by Oswald Chambers. Copyright © 1935 by Doug Mead & Co., renewed © 1963 by the Oswald Chambers Publications Assn. Ltd., and is used by permission of Discovery House Publishers, Box 3566, Grand Rapids, MI 49501. All rights reserved.
2. Elisabeth Elliot, *A Chance to Die* (Grand Rapids, MI: Fleming H. Revell, 1987), 31.
3. Chambers, *My Utmost for His Highest,* 58.
4. Chambers, *My Utmost for His Highest,* 73.

Chapter 5

1. Eric Ludy, *Meet Mr. Smith* (Nashville: Thomas Nelson, 2007), 179–180.

Chapter 6

1. Chuck Colson, "Any Old World View Will Do," *Perspective,* May 1998.

Chapter 7

1. Leslie Ludy, *Authentic Beauty* (Colorado Springs: Multnomah, 2003), 168.

Chapter 8

1. Richard Lattimore, *Homer's Odyssey* (New York: Harper and Row, 1950), 305–328.
2. Oswald Chambers, *My Utmost for His Highest* (Uhrichsville, OH: Barbour Publishing, 1935), 129.

3. J. R. Miller as quoted in Mrs. Charles E. Cowman, *Streams in the Desert* (Grand Rapids, MI: Zondervan, 1984), 195.

Chapter 9

1. John Ruskin as quoted in Mrs. Charles E. Cowman, *Streams in the Desert* (Grand Rapids, MI: Zondervan, 1984), 33.
2. Leslie Ludy, *Authentic Beauty* (Colorado Springs: Multnomah, 2003), 76–77.
3. Ludy, *Authentic Beauty,* 75.
4. Cowman, *Streams in the Desert,* 216.

Chapter 10

1. Leslie Ludy, *Answering the Guy Questions* (Eugene, OR: Harvest House, 2009), 75–76.
2. Adapted from S. I. Kishor, "Appointment with Love," *Collier's,* June 5, 1943, 15.
3. Oswald Chambers, *My Utmost for His Highest* (Uhrichsville, OH: Barbour Publishing, 1935), 53.

Chapter 11

1. Phillips Brooks as quoted in Mrs. Charles E. Cowman, *Streams in the Desert* (Grand Rapids, MI: Zondervan, 1984), 243.
2. Corrie ten Boom, *Tramp for the Lord* (New York: Jove/Penguin Putnam, 1978), 55.

Chapter 12

1. As quoted in Mrs. Charles E. Cowman, *Streams in the Desert* (Grand Rapids, MI: Zondervan, 1984), 239.

Chapter 14

1. Michael Card, *The Parable of Joy* (Nashville: Thomas Nelson, 1995), 103–105. (Michael Card's rendering of John 8:1–11.)
2. Card, 107.
3. Frederick Buechner as quoted in Card, 104.
4. Oswald Chambers, *My Utmost for His Highest* (Uhrichsville, OH: Barbour Publishing, 1935), 366.
5. As quoted in Carole C. Carlson, *Corrie ten Boom—Her Life, Her Faith* (New Jersey: Revell, 1983), 159–160.

Chapter 15

1. Eric Ludy, *God's Gift to Women* (Colorado Springs: Multnomah, 2003), 107.
2. A. W. Tozer, *The Pursuit of God* (Camp Hill, PA: Christian Publication, 1993), 23.
3. Oswald Chambers, *My Utmost for His Highest* (Uhrichsville, OH: Barbour Publishing, 1935), 129.
4. George Mueller as quoted by Mrs. Charles E. Cowman, *Streams in the Desert* (Grand Rapids, MI: Zondervan, 1984), 140.
5. Chambers, *My Utmost for His Highest,* 336.
6. Henry Blackaby, *Experiencing God* (Nashville: Lifeway Press, 1990), 19.
7. Chambers, *My Utmost for His Highest,* 58.

Relationship Q&A

1. Leslie Ludy, *Set-Apart Femininity* (Eugene, OR: Harvest House, 2008), 116.

WONDERING WHERE TO GO FROM HERE?

WANT TO TAKE THIS MESSAGE EVEN DEEPER IN YOUR LIFE?

We would love to connect with you!

www.SETAPARTLIFE.com

Visit our website for details about our new books, events and ministry plans - as well as our blogs, podcasts, videos and resources designed to encourage you down the narrow way of the Cross.

Hope to see you there!

Eric & Leslie

The perfect follow-up to
When God Writes Your Love Story:

When Dreams Come True

Eric and Leslie's love story captured in a
powerful, novel-style narrative that will
grip you from start to finish!

This daringly real, intensely moving love story gives vision and hope to everyone in search of a love worth waiting for. In their bestseller *When God Writes Your Love Story*, Eric and Leslie Ludy describe the breathtaking perfection of God's plans for each young person and offer fresh guidelines for being Christlike in relationships with the opposite sex. *When Dreams Come True* shares the Ludy's personal story, illustrating how they lived out the principles of the first book in their own romance and marriage.

WHEN DREAMS
COME TRUE

a love story
only God could write

Eric & Leslie Ludy

More great books by authors

ERIC & LESLIE LUDY

AUTHENTIC BEAUTY

In a world that seeks to destroy all that is truly feminine within us; in a culture that exalts selfishness and sensuality and mocks our longing for a fairy tale romance - can we dare to long for more? For every young woman asking that question, this book offers a breathtaking vision of hope. Refreshingly candid and practical, *Authentic Beauty* explores the boundless opportunities God has for the life of a young woman who is willing to let Him shape every aspect of her existence.

WHEN GOD WRITES YOUR LIFE STORY

Whether you're currently tackling major life decisions or simply longing to live a life that really counts, *When God Writes Your Life Story* will infuse you with vision and purpose. This book introduces the amazing journey that awaits us when we step into God's endless frontier. It showcases the heroic potential of the true Christian life. The God of the Universe wants to write your life story. And when He does, you mustn't expect a mediocre tale!

GOD'S GIFT TO WOMEN
- Discovering the Lost Greatness of Masculinity

Deep within the rugged soul of every young man, there is a warrior in search of his sword and a poet in search of his pen. But heroic masculinity is something most women only dream of in today's perverse and self-serving world. With contagious passion and boldness, Eric Ludy challenges young men to exchange male mediocrity for Christ-built, warrior-poet manhood that will capture the heart of a woman and change the course of history.